P9-DMK-373

THE ART OF WOODWORKING

MASTER WOODWORKER

THE ART OF WOODWORKING

MASTER WOODWORKER

TIME-LIFE BOOKS
ALEXANDRIA, VIRGINIA

ST. REMY PRESS
MONTREAL • NEW YORK

THE ART OF WOODWORKING was produced by
ST. REMY PRESS

PUBLISHER	Kenneth Winchester
PRESIDENT	Pierre Léveillé
Series Editor	Pierre Home-Douglas
Series Art Director	Francine Lemieux
Senior Editors	Marc Cassini (Text)
	Heather Mills (Research)
Art Directors	Normand Boudreault, Luc Germain,
	Solange Laberge
Designers	Lina Desrochers, Jean-Guy Doiron,
	Michel Giguère
Research Editor	Jim McRae
Picture Editor	Christopher Jackson
Writers	Andrew Jones, Rob Lutes
Research Assistant	Bryan Quinn
Contributing Illustrators	Gilles Beauchemin, Roland Bergerat,
	Michel Blais, Jean-Pierre Bourgeois,
	Ronald Durepos, Jacques Perrault,
	James Thérien
Administrator	Natalie Watanabe
Production Manager	Michelle Turbide
System Coordinator	Jean-Luc Roy
Photographers	Robert Chartier, Christian Levesque
Administrative Assistant	Dominique Gagné
Proofreader	Judith Yelon
Indexer	Christine M. Jacobs

Time-Life Books is a division of Time Life Inc.,
a wholly owned subsidiary of
THE TIME INC. BOOK COMPANY

TIME LIFE INC.

President and CEO	John M. Fahey
Editor-in-chief	John L. Papanek

TIME-LIFE BOOKS

President	John D. Hall
Vice-President, Director of Marketing	Nancy K. Jones
Executive Editor	Roberta Conlan
Executive Art Director	Ellen Robling
Consulting Editor	John R. Sullivan
Production Manager	Marlene Zack

THE CONSULTANTS

Ian Agrell, a British Master Carver, has been carving for 33 years. He teaches at The School of Classical Woodcarving in Sausalito, California. He and Adam Thorpe also run Agrell and Thorpe, Ltd., a shop that produces carving works and furniture.

Jon Arno is a consultant, cabinetmaker, and freelance writer who lives in Troy, Michigan. He also conducts seminars on wood identification and early American furniture design.

Michael Fortune of Toronto, Canada, has been designing and building furniture for 19 years for private residences in both Canada and the United States. He also travels throughout North America giving lectures on wood forming and furniture design and construction.

Silas Kopf has been building furniture and decorating it with marquetry for two decades. He currently runs Silas Kopf Woodworking Inc., in Northampton, Massachusetts.

Drew Langsner of Marshall, North Carolina, has been working green wood for 22 years. He produces traditionally made ladder-back and Windsor chairs, and is the director of Country Workshops, where he teaches courses and sells specialty tools.

Giles Miller-Mead taught advanced cabinetmaking at Montreal technical schools for more than ten years. A native of New Zealand, he has worked as a restorer of antique furniture.

Master woodworker
 p. cm.—(The Art of Woodworking)
Includes index.
ISBN 0-8094-9504-X
1. Woodwork—Amateurs' manuals
I. Time-Life Books.
II. Series.
TT185.M34 1994
674'.8—dc20   93-41959
                                CIP

For information about any Time-Life book,
please call 1-800-621-7026, or write:
Reader Information
Time-Life Customer Service
P.O. Box C-32068
Richmond, Virginia
23261-2068

© 1994 Time-Life Books Inc.
All rights reserved.
No part of this book may be reproduced in any form or by any electronic or mechanical means, including information storage and retrieval devices or systems, without prior written permission from the publisher, except that brief passages may be quoted for reviews.
First printing. Printed in U.S.A.
Published simultaneously in Canada.

TIME-LIFE is a trademark of Time Warner Inc. U.S.A.

CONTENTS

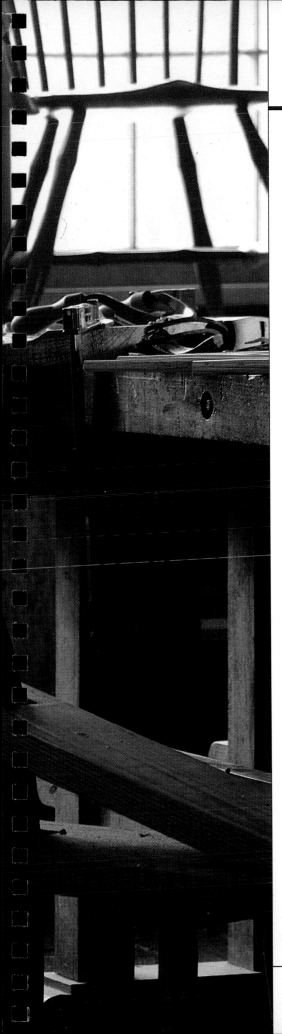

Drew Langsner discusses

WORKING GREEN WOOD

I first became interested in traditional woodworking in 1972 while traveling in the Swiss Alps. I spent a few days at a remote Alpine cabin and the nearest neighbor was a herder and cheese maker whose milk and cream containers were old and very beautiful. The tubs and buckets were coopered and held together with perfectly crafted wooden hoops. These containers were still being made by an old man in the area, Reudi Kohler. His workshop was a converted horse stall on the ground level of the 19th Century chalet where he lived. The shop was about 10 feet wide and 20 feet deep. Along one wall was a massive, homemade joiner's workbench. Front and center was his shaving horse. He also had an old 30-inch band saw, a wood lathe, and a huge combination planer/jointer/table saw. The shelving above his bench was filled with well-used hand tools. On the opposite wall was a display cabinet with examples of his craft for sale.

Several weeks after my first visit, I returned to Kohler's shop to ask if he would consider taking on an apprentice. To my surprise, he agreed. I spent that summer learning the rudiments of a very challenging craft: using the splitting froe, broad hatchet, various drawknives, spokeshaves, and a variety of other simple hand tools that are used to work wood directly from a tree.

My workshop in the mountains of North Carolina is similar to my teacher's. I now have a Swiss workbench, and an excellent selection of very good hand tools. The seat of my shaving horse—the one I am using to drawknife a chair rung in the photo—is polished from more than 20 years of use. Like my teacher, I also use machinery to free up time for hand-tool work, which is where I find real enjoyment.

Although I started out learning cooperage, I now make ladderback and Windsor chairs, and I enjoy carving spoons and large bowls in the Scandinavian tradition. With each of these crafts, I began working in a conservative, traditional way. But gradually, as I gained skill and an understanding of why the old patterns were followed in a particular way, I began to develop my own design variations. I have the highest respect for the master woodworkers of the past. But at the same time I also want to make my own contribution to the crafts that have meant so much to me.

Drew Langsner of Marshall, North Carolina, is the author of books and articles on green woodworking. He also runs Country Workshops, offering classes on chair making, coopering, and Swedish woodenware.

Michael Fortune on

BENDING WOOD

M ost of the wood we use to make furniture is sawn into rectilinear planks from trees that are anything but rectilinear. The boards are virtually extruded from the tree "straight and true" with little regard for grain direction. Creating interesting furniture from the boards multiplies the problem as we saw curves and shapes, often creating weak cross-grain components.

The product of this method often fails: The chair leg, for example, that breaks because its curved shape cuts across the grain of the board from which it was sawn. Cutting the shapes we need from tree branches is one answer but somewhat impractical nowadays—especially when the tree with just the right crook is probably growing in your neighbor's front yard!

Another answer is to bend the wood to the shape you need. One of the pioneers in that field was a European cabinetmaker named Michael Thonet, who mass produced bentwood chairs at the turn of the 20th Century. Years of trial and error eventually led Thonet to discover the key elements that allowed wood to be bent with great success. Those basics are explained in the bending chapter starting on page 40. The chapter also explains other wood-forming techniques such as strip laminating and forming wide panels, which actually make the wood dramatically stronger than the original individual pieces. The technique of coopering—joining boards edge to edge to create curves—is also illustrated.

There is a mystery surrounding the process of bending wood. Some people try it and find it virtually impossible. But once you have mastered some basic techniques, your desire to reproduce timeless antiques or execute imaginative new designs will not be limited to the shape of boards in the lumberyard. Making a graceful *and* strong chair leg, a curved table apron, or a bow front cabinet will all be within your command.

Good luck in your projects. I hope you find wood forming as rewarding as I have.

Michael Fortune is a Toronto-based furniture designer who lectures throughout North America. His work earned him the 1993 Saidye Bronfman Award. Fortune's works are featured in the permanent collection of The Canadian Museum of Civilization.

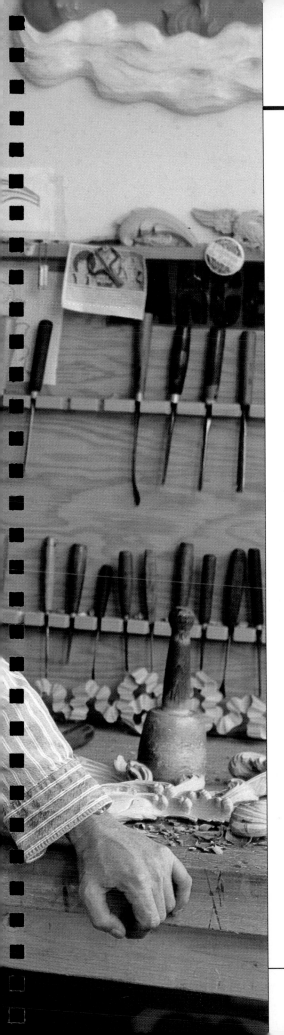

Ian Agrell talks about
CARVING

When I was sixteen and in the British Army, I was told that I had to develop a hobby. It was the freezing winter of 1962 and I didn't fancy playing soccer outside. I had always enjoyed art projects in school, and so with the knowledge that the art class had a particularly large furnace, I started my carving career. My first project was a ferret carved in pine. This was followed by other animals worked in wood, alabaster, and even soap.

Later, when I wanted to make my living as a carver, I decided that I had better broaden my knowledge of the craft. Classical carving—modeling works on the architecture and decoration of ancient Greece—was the logical place to start. It is an essential skill of a professional carver.

I was trained in London by some of the older master carvers. These men came from a long tradition of artisans who guarded the secrets of carving very closely. It was tough prying little hints and tips from them. But, together with other students wishing to learn from the masters, I managed, and tried to save the knowledge to pass on to the next generation of carvers.

As a carver, you need to have a clear understanding of your project before a chisel touches the wood. This should be accomplished by drawing, modeling, or copying an object. I am not in the business of "feeling" my way in as artists do when they create original works. In my shop, we must accurately estimate the time and materials needed to produce the highest quality product and deliver it on time.

Study the underlying structure of the piece that you are carving. Observe the contours and carve them accurately. Don't get confused by all the details and start carving them until you are sure the skeleton of the work is in place. The movement and flow of a carving will distinguish a good carver—one who has an understanding of the medium. Observe the movement of the clothes on a twisting body or a flame licking up a chimney and use these observations in your work. The same law applies whether you are carving an acanthus leaf or an otter chasing a salmon.

Ultimately, a carver uses his skills to recreate in wood what he sees in the world. Consequently, a good carver is one who is constantly learning to observe.

Ian Agrell was elected to the Association of British Master Carvers in 1981 and is now the principal instructor at The School of Classical Woodcarving in Sausalito, California. His workshop also undertakes furniture-making and carving projects.

Silas Kopf discusses
MARQUETRY

Woodworking is a complex craft with many different aspects, and I suspect that marquetry can appear to be impossibly difficult to the novice. In learning to build furniture I concentrated on joinery and solid wood construction. But after a while I started to pay attention to historic furniture and wondered how certain design elements were accomplished. I had a particular interest in the turn-of-the-century French Art Nouveau furniture of designer Emile Gallé and cabinetmaker Louis Majorelle, which used marquetry decoration. Eventually I became aware of Italian Renaissance woodwork and 18th-Century French furniture, which also relied heavily on marquetry.

My goal with marquetry is to incorporate a pictographic design into a piece of furniture so that both are enhanced. The decoration is often the focus of the piece, but the design will ideally lead the viewer into the form and function of the whole. It is important to me to "celebrate" the fact that the piece is being done with wood. The dining room sideboard shown in the photo is made of mahogany with imbuya as the main wood in the marquetry—a cardinal motif.

Most of my marquetry is cut on a scroll saw using a technique called double-bevel cutting. One piece of veneer is laid on top of another and the two pieces are cut at the same time. Every cut then has two pieces of wood that fit together and two waste pieces. The sawing is done at an angle so the piece on top is slightly larger than the piece below, and when they end up on the same plane the gap left by the saw kerf is eliminated. The two pieces of veneer are then taped together. The design is transferred to the work and the next piece of the picture is added in the same way. This process is repeated— cut, tape, draw, cut, tape, draw—until the entire picture is assembled. It is then treated like any other sheet of veneer, to be glued and incorporated into the furniture.

Marquetry and complex veneering can be used to advantage by designers and craftsmen alike. We can distinguish our work and provide that element of individual "personality" to a piece of furniture. My advice to others would be to look at antiques, experiment, and have fun.

Silas Kopf has practiced marquetry for 18 of his 20 years as a woodworker. He studied at Ecole Boulle in Paris under master marqueteur Pierre Ramond. He now runs a woodworking shop in Northampton, Massachusetts.

WORKING GREEN WOOD

In an era of kiln-dried lumber and power tools, working freshly cut wood seems more than a little whimsical—a throwback to a bygone era when itinerant woodcarvers, turners, and chair-makers would travel from town to town, sizing up the trees and the local demand for hayforks, barrels, bowls, chairs, shingles, and baskets. In England in the late 19th Century, craftsmen known as chair bodgers would set up shop just outside town. The surrounding trees provided the bodger with all the raw materials for his mill, shop, and home. Starting with a minimal tool kit, he could fashion many of the other tools necessary to fell, split, and shape local trees: items like clubs, gluts, tool handles, a pole lathe powered by a treadle, and the heart of the green woodshop, the shaving horse *(page 26)*. Some of the tools used in the modern green woodworker's shop are shown beginning on page 16.

Today, revivalist movements in England and North America have rediscovered the simple, elegant tradition of green woodworking. Yet there is more to working green wood than simple nostalgia; there are a number of good reasons to work with wood from freshly felled

Windsor chair making is one craft tailor-made for green woodworking. Most of the elements of the example shown above—the legs, spindles, stretcher, rungs, and continuous arm—were riven and shaped from green wood by North Carolina woodworker Drew Langsner.

trees. Because the wood is swollen with moisture, it splits, cleaves, and bends more easily than dried wood. It is also softer and easier to shape with drawknives, spokeshaves, and other hand tools. Second, cleaving wood from a log yields wood of greater strength because the break follows the wood fibers rather than shearing them, as a sawmill does. Third, wood seasons, or dries, better if it is shaped while still green. A cylindrical chair rung will season more quickly and be less prone to cracking than a board, which may cup or check. Last but not least, the quiet cleanliness of working green wood by hand is a refreshing departure from the din and dust of the modern woodshop.

The chapter that follows takes you through the craft of green woodworking, from the basics of felling and harvesting a tree *(page 22)*, to cleaving, or riving, stock from the log *(page 24)*, and shaping the stock into a finished project *(page 30)*. Along the way, you will discover that following a tree's unique shape and form will help you produce equally individual finished pieces. And, as green woodworking proponents are quick to add, you may also experience a more relaxed way of working with wood.

A single log can usually furnish all the wood needed for a chair or stool—often with plenty to spare. At left, a bowsaw cuts a blank for a stool seat from a poplar log. The blank will later be shaped with a variety of tools. See page 29 for a photo of the finished stool.

GREEN WOODWORKING TOOLS

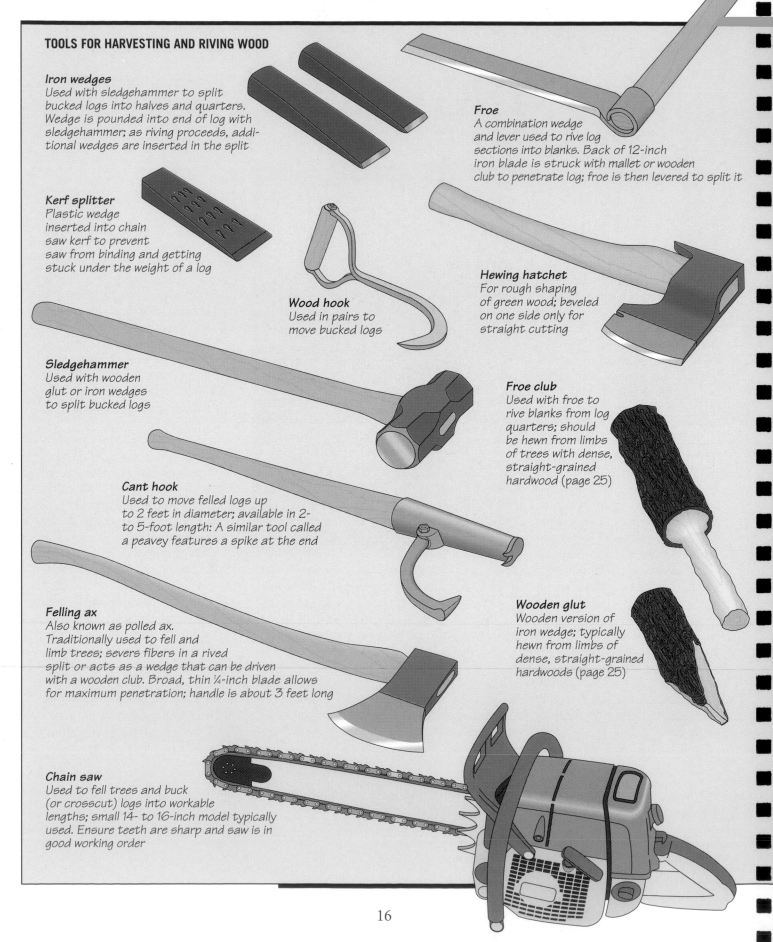

TOOLS FOR HARVESTING AND RIVING WOOD

Iron wedges
Used with sledgehammer to split bucked logs into halves and quarters. Wedge is pounded into end of log with sledgehammer; as riving proceeds, additional wedges are inserted in the split

Kerf splitter
Plastic wedge inserted into chain saw kerf to prevent saw from binding and getting stuck under the weight of a log

Sledgehammer
Used with wooden glut or iron wedges to split bucked logs

Cant hook
Used to move felled logs up to 2 feet in diameter; available in 2- to 5-foot length: A similar tool called a peavey features a spike at the end

Felling ax
Also known as polled ax. Traditionally used to fell and limb trees; severs fibers in a rived split or acts as a wedge that can be driven with a wooden club. Broad, thin ¼-inch blade allows for maximum penetration; handle is about 3 feet long

Chain saw
Used to fell trees and buck (or crosscut) logs into workable lengths; small 14- to 16-inch model typically used. Ensure teeth are sharp and saw is in good working order

Froe
A combination wedge and lever used to rive log sections into blanks. Back of 12-inch iron blade is struck with mallet or wooden club to penetrate log; froe is then levered to split it

Wood hook
Used in pairs to move bucked logs

Hewing hatchet
For rough shaping of green wood; beveled on one side only for straight cutting

Froe club
Used with froe to rive blanks from log quarters; should be hewn from limbs of trees with dense, straight-grained hardwood (page 25)

Wooden glut
Wooden version of iron wedge; typically hewn from limbs of dense, straight-grained hardwoods (page 25)

STOCK PREPARATION AND BORING TOOLS

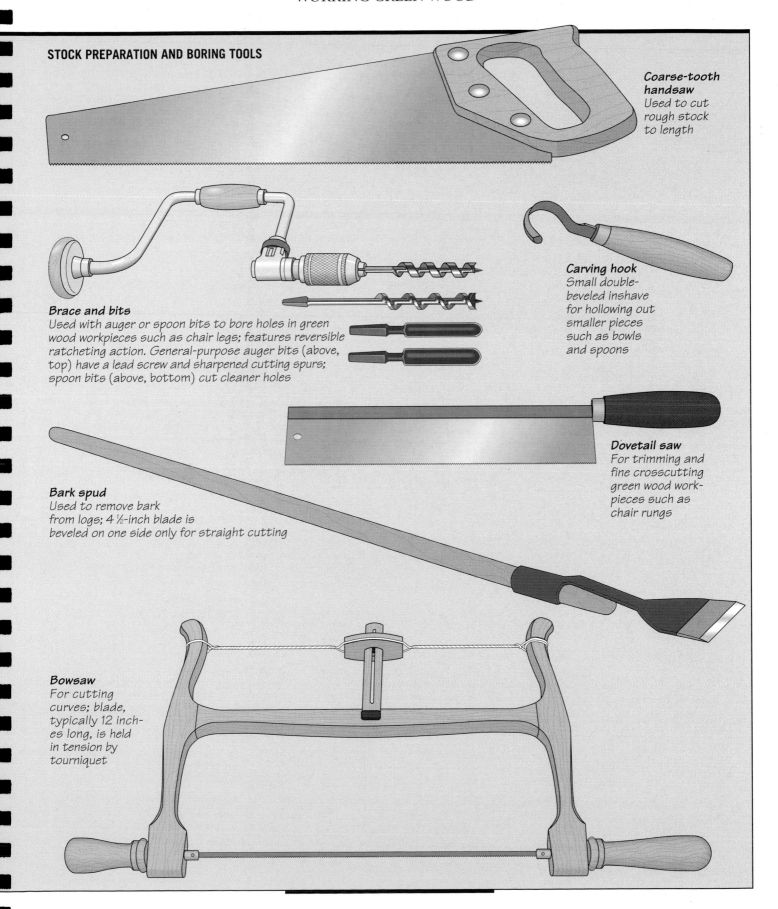

Coarse-tooth handsaw
Used to cut rough stock to length

Carving hook
Small double-beveled inshave for hollowing out smaller pieces such as bowls and spoons

Brace and bits
Used with auger or spoon bits to bore holes in green wood workpieces such as chair legs; features reversible ratcheting action. General-purpose auger bits (above, top) have a lead screw and sharpened cutting spurs; spoon bits (above, bottom) cut cleaner holes

Dovetail saw
For trimming and fine crosscutting green wood workpieces such as chair rungs

Bark spud
Used to remove bark from logs; 4½-inch blade is beveled on one side only for straight cutting

Bowsaw
For cutting curves; blade, typically 12 inches long, is held in tension by tourniquet

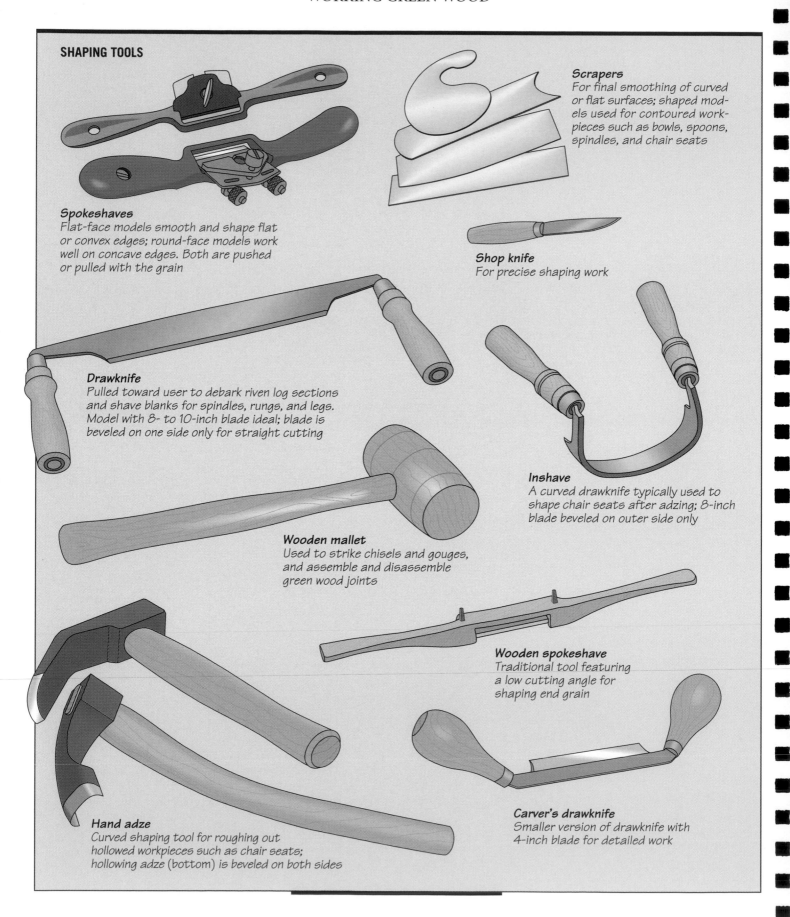

SHAPING TOOLS

Scrapers
For final smoothing of curved or flat surfaces; shaped models used for contoured workpieces such as bowls, spoons, spindles, and chair seats

Spokeshaves
Flat-face models smooth and shape flat or convex edges; round-face models work well on concave edges. Both are pushed or pulled with the grain

Shop knife
For precise shaping work

Drawknife
Pulled toward user to debark riven log sections and shave blanks for spindles, rungs, and legs. Model with 8- to 10-inch blade ideal; blade is beveled on one side only for straight cutting

Inshave
A curved drawknife typically used to shape chair seats after adzing; 8-inch blade beveled on outer side only

Wooden mallet
Used to strike chisels and gouges, and assemble and disassemble green wood joints

Wooden spokeshave
Traditional tool featuring a low cutting angle for shaping end grain

Hand adze
Curved shaping tool for roughing out hollowed workpieces such as chair seats; hollowing adze (bottom) is beveled on both sides

Carver's drawknife
Smaller version of drawknife with 4-inch blade for detailed work

Although the polled ax was the bodger's tool-of-choice for felling trees, modern green woodworkers prefer to use a chain saw. Whatever the size of the tree you decide to cut down, be sure to follow the chain saw manufacturer's instructions and the precautions outlined in the box below. Trees are heavy, and cutting one down improperly can prove dangerous or even deadly. The techniques for felling a tree are shown beginning on page 22. If you do not have access to a woodlot, you may be able to get freshly cut logs from a sawmill, a local firewood supplier, or your local roads department.

When choosing a log that has already been felled, avoid those with twisted or wavy grain, or with many knots; these will be difficult to rive. Steer clear of logs containing rot or stain. With some hardwoods, you can gauge the strength of the wood by examining the growth rings. Narrow growth rings signify slower growth and weaker wood. Curiously, the opposite holds true for softwoods. Try to determine when the tree was felled; the more recently, the better. There are many conflicting views about the ideal time of year to fell trees; but it is certain that you should harvest a tree as close as possible to the time you will use it.

The charts on pages 20 and 21 on the workability and riving quality of various woods will help you choose an appropriate species for your projects.

If you wish to store green wood for future projects, stack the logs outside, raised off the ground, and in the shade. Coat the end grain with a sealer to prevent checking. For long-term storage, you can submerge the wood in a large drum of water to prevent it from drying out or rotting.

Once a log is bucked into workable lengths, the next step is to split it in two. Here, a sledgehammer drives an iron wedge into the log end, separating the wood fibers along the grain. Always wear eye protection when striking metal against metal.

SELECTING TIMBER

TIPS ON CHOOSING AND FELLING A TREE

• Never try to fell a tree alone; work with a helper.

• Always wear steel-toed work boots and a hard hat for protection. Do not wear loose clothing that could catch in limbs.

• Do not fell timber in windy conditions; you will not have proper control over the tree as it falls.

• Avoid trees that grow on steep slopes; the forces necessary to counteract gravity distort the tree's cells and produce reaction wood that can cause kickback.

• Look for trees that grow in the shade. Such trees grow taller and lose their lower limbs more quickly than those in the open sun, resulting in wood with straighter grain and fewer knots.

• Select a straight-standing specimen free of knots, twists, and insect holes for felling.

• When selecting logs at a sawmill, examine the growth rings and look for fast-growing hardwoods or slow-growing softwoods.

• Read the bark. Bark that spirals upward around a tree trunk is a good indication that the grain of the wood underneath will do likewise and rive into twisted parts; knobby bark is a sign of buried knots.

• Check the lean of a tree and the distribution of its limbs. If the tree is leaning heavily, or the limbs are weighted in one direction, plan to fell it at a right angle to that direction.

WORKABILITY OF VARIOUS WOODS

HARD

- Apple *(Malus pumila)*
- Ash *(Fraxinus spp.)*
- Beech *(Fagus grandifolia)*
- Birch, white *(Betula papyrifera)*
- Birch, yellow *(Betula alleghaniensis)*
- Cedar, Eastern red *(Juniperus virginiana)*
- Cherry, wild *(Prunus serotina)*
- Dogwood *(Cornus florida)*
- Elm *(Ulmus spp.)*
- Gum, black *(Nyssa sylvatica)*
- Hackberry *(Celtis occidentalis)*
- Hickory *(Carya spp.)*
- Holly *(Ilex opaca)*
- Hornbeam, American *(Carpinus caroliniana)*
- Larch, Western *(Larix occidentalis)*
- Lilac *(Syringa spp.)*
- Locust, black *(Robinia pseudoacacia)*
- Locust, honey *(Gleditsia triacanthos)*
- Maple *(Acer spp.)*
- Mesquite *(Prosopis spp.)*
- Oak *(Quercus spp.)*
- Olive *(Olea europea)*
- Osage orange *(Maclura pomifera)*
- Pear *(Pyrus spp.)*
- Pecan *(Carya illinoensis)*
- Persimmon *(Diospyros virginiana)*
- Pine, Southern yellow *(Pinus spp.)*
- Sycamore *(Platanus occidentalis)*
- Yew, Pacific *(Taxus brevifolia)*

INTERMEDIATE

- Alder *(Alnus spp.)*
- Baldcypress *(Taxodium spp.)*
- Chestnut *(Castanea dentata)*
- Douglas-fir *(Psudotsuga menziesii)*
- Gum, red *(Liquidambar styraciflua)*
- Hemlock *(Tsuga spp.)*
- Mulberry *(Morus spp.)*
- Redwood *(Sequoia sempervirens)*
- Sassafras *(Sassafras albidum)*
- Spruce *(Picea spp.)*

SOFT

- Aspen *(Populus spp.)*
- Basswood *(Tilia americana)*
- Buckeye *(Aesculus spp.)*
- Butternut *(Juglans cinerea)*
- Catalpa *(Catalpa spp.)*
- Cedar, Northern white *(Thuja occidentalis)*
- Cedar, Southern white *(Chamaecyparis thyoides)*
- Cedar, Western red *(Thujaplicata)*
- Cottonwood *(Populus spp.)*
- Fir, true *(Abies spp.)*
- Magnolia *(Magnolia spp.)*
- Pine, Northern white *(Pinus strobus)*
- Pine, ponderosa *(Pinus ponderosa)*
- Pine, sugar *(Pinus lambertiana)*
- Pine, Western white *(Pinus monticola)*
- Poplar, yellow *(Liriodendron tulipifera)*
- Tupelo, water *(Nyssa aquatica)*
- Willow *(Salix spp.)*

Hardness in green wood

The chart above rates a variety of woods in terms of their relative hardness. This quality is double-edged. What makes a wood durable and long-lasting also makes it difficult to work with hand tools. But even a very hard wood like hickory, a traditional favorite for tool handles, is much softer and easier to work when it is green. Ash is another popular green wood; it is often used in chair-making because it is lightweight yet very shock-resistant. While hardness is important, it should not be the only variable you consider. The eventual use of the wood should be the overriding factor. For example, the pores of white oak have an impervious quality that make this wood prized for casks used to age whiskey and bourbon. Black locust, which resists decay, has traditionally been used for fence posts.

Chart courtesy of Drew Langsner

RIVING QUALITIES OF VARIOUS WOODS

GOOD TO EXCELLENT
- Ash *(Fraxinus spp.)*
- Baldcypress *(Taxodium spp.)*
- Butternut *(Juglans cinerea)*
- Cedar, Northern white *(Thuja occidentalis)*
- Cedar, Western red *(Thuja plicata)*
- Chestnut *(Castanea dentata)*
- Hackberry *(Celtis occidentalis)*
- Hemlock *(Tsuga spp.)*
- Hickory *(Carya spp.)*
- Larch *(Larix spp.)*
- Locust, black *(Robinia pseudoacacia)*
- Locust, honey *(Gleditsia triacanthos)*
- Maple, soft *(Acer rubrum)*
- Oak, red *(Quercus rubra)*
- Oak, white *(Quercus alba)*
- Osage orange *(Maclura pomifera)*
- Pecan *(Carya illinoensis)*
- Pine, Eastern white *(Pinus strobus)*
- Redwood *(Sequoia sempervirens)*
- Spruce *(Picea spp.)*
- Walnut *(Juglans spp.)*
- Willow *(Salix spp.)*

FAIR
- Apple *(Malus pumila)*
- Basswood *(Tilia americana)*
- Beech *(Fagus grandifolia)*
- Birch *(Betula spp.)*
- Buckeye *(Aesculus spp.)*
- Catalpa *(Catalpa spp.)*
- Cedar, Eastern red *(Juniperus virginiana)*
- Cherry *(Prunus spp.)*
- Cottonwood *(Populus spp.)*
- Dogwood *(Cornus florida)*
- Douglas-fir *(Pseudotsuga menziesii)*
- Holly *(Ilex opaca)*
- Magnolia *(Magnolia spp.)*
- Maple, hard *(Acer saccharum)*
- Mulberry *(Morus spp.)*
- Oak, live *(Quercus virginiana)*
- Pear *(Pyrus spp.)*
- Pine, Southern yellow *(Pinus spp.)*
- Poplar, yellow *(Liriodendron tulipifera)*
- Sumac *(Rhus spp.)*
- Sycamore *(Platanus occidentalis)*

POOR
- Elm *(Ulmus spp.)*
- Eucalyptus *(Eucalyptus spp.)*
- Gum, black *(Nyssa sylvatica)*
- Hornbeam, American *(Carpinus caroliniana)*
- Oak, swamp *(Quercus bicolor)*
- Persimmon *(Diospyros virginiana)*

Chart courtesy of Drew Langsner

Figure in green wood
The chart on this page compares the riving qualities of various species. Riving quality, or how readily the timber will split along the grain with a wedge or froe *(page 24)*, is directly related to the wood's figure, or grain pattern. As with hardness, selecting a wood on the basis of its riving quality is not a clear-cut process. While dense woods such as beech and hornbeam will not split as predictably or easily as white oak, hickory, or ash, their appealing figure makes them ideal for many uses. And not every green woodworking project calls for riving large logs into long workpieces; short limbs or trunk sections of difficult species with appealing figure, such as apple, basswood, and holly, can be harvested for bowls, spoons, and smaller carving or turning projects.

HARVESTING A LOG

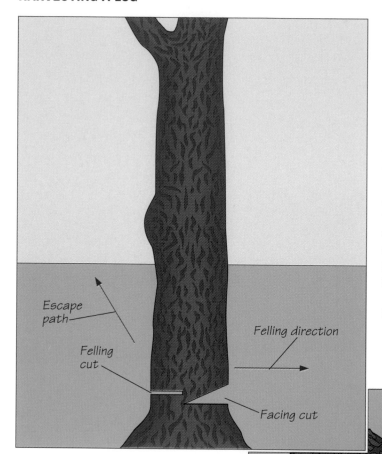

Escape
path

Felling
cut

Felling direction

Facing cut

1 Felling the tree
Once you have selected a tree and the felling direction, examine the surrounding trees and make sure they will not snag your chosen tree. Check that there are no loose limbs—known as widow-makers—about to fall. Also choose an escape path; it should be at roughly a right angle to the tree's felling direction. As shown at left, fell the tree by making two cuts, starting with the facing cut, which is done in two steps. The first is a cut made about halfway straight through the trunk on the side facing the direction in which the tree should fall. Next, make a cut starting slightly higher up the trunk and angling down at 30° to 45° to meet the first cut. Then make the felling cut on the opposite side of the tree a couple of inches above the facing cut. The felling cut should stop an inch or two from the facing cut to leave a hinge that will prevent the tree from kicking back. Once the tree begins to move, quickly remove the saw and follow your escape path. If the tree becomes lodged or will not fall, leave the area immediately and get experienced help.

2 Bucking the log
Once you have felled the log and trimmed off the branches, you need to buck it into workable lengths. Prop the log up on branches or small logs so that the chain saw blade will not hit the ground and the cut piece will be free to fall. Then saw the log into bolts, or lengths, that suit the needs of your project *(right)*. Start at the bottom of the tree, which is the area with the straightest and most knot-free wood.

3 Splitting the bolt into halves and quarters

Whether or not you are using the wood immediately, it is best to split the bolt into quarters before storing it; this will prevent radial shrinkage and checking. Do the job with a sledgehammer and iron wedges, making sure to wear eye protection throughout the operation. First, stand the bolt up, mark the center on one end, and drive a wedge into the mark. Once the bolt begins to split—and this may take a few sledgehammer blows—turn the bolt onto its side. Drive a second wedge into the split and strike it with the sledgehammer *(right)*. Continue driving the wedge until the log breaks in two. (For longer bolts, you may need to remove the first wedge, drive it in behind the second, and repeat this leapfrogging process until the bolt splits in half.) Repeat the procedure to split the halves into quarters *(below)*.

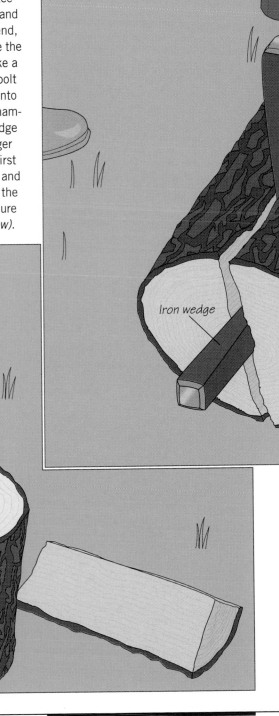

Iron wedge

RIVING WOOD BLANKS

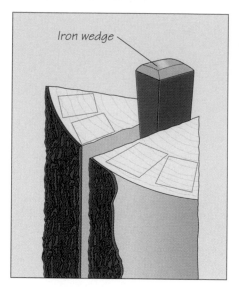

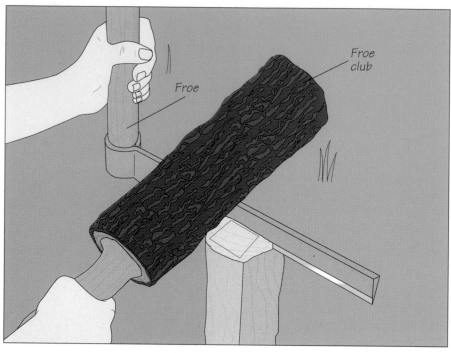

1 Riving a quarter bolt into blanks
Once you have split a bolt into quarters, rive each piece into blanks of the appropriate size for your project. First, outline the blanks on the end of the workpiece and split it *(above, left)*, using the same technique used to halve and quarter logs *(page 23)*. The blanks are then riven with a froe and froe club. (If the piece is small, you may be able to dispense with the wedge and sledgehammer and do all the riving with the froe.) Holding the froe in one hand with the blade set back a bit from the marked line, strike the blade with the club. Twist the froe back and forth, and drive it in deeper. Once the waste breaks off, repeat to make the remaining cuts *(above, right)*.

Riving green wood with a froe and froe club is one of the basic procedures of green woodworking. The break will follow the wood fibers rather than shear them, resulting in stronger, more durable workpieces. In the photo at right, the log section is held at a convenient angle by a brake, made from a tree crotch. Two branches crossing through the crotch in an X hold up the brake and support the log at the desired angle.

BUILD IT YOURSELF

A WOODEN GLUT AND FROE CLUB

Instead of splitting and riving green wood with metal tools, you can make your own wooden implements from small logs. The glut *(near right)* can be used in place of an iron wedge, while the club can be used to strike a froe. Make two gluts from a single limb; it should be about 24 inches long and 3½ inches in diameter. Use a hewing hatchet to taper both ends at an angle of about 20° *(far right)*, then cut the limb in half.

Make the club from a 16- to 18-inch length of dense hardwood, such as maple, dogwood, hickory, or elm. The limb should be about 4 inches in diameter and ideally have plenty of knots at the end that will form the head to give it strength. Starting about 10 inches from one end, use a bowsaw to cut to a depth of about 1 inch all around the log. Then use

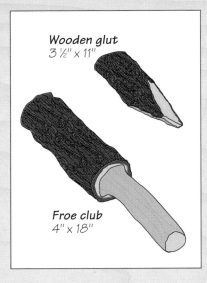

Wooden glut
3 ½" x 11"

Froe club
4" x 18"

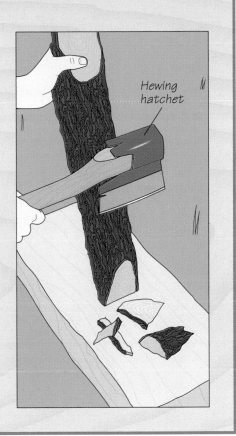

Hewing hatchet

a hewing hatchet to chop out the waste between this cut and the end, forming a handle.

To prevent the wood from checking, let the gluts and club dry slowly in a cool, humid location.

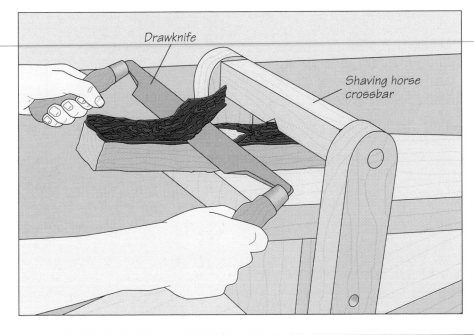

Drawknife

Shaving horse crossbar

2 Debarking the blanks
Remove bark from your blanks on a shaving horse that you can build in the shop *(page 26)*. Secure each blank bark-side up under the horse's crossbar. Then, holding a drawknife in both hands with the blade bevel down, pull the tool toward you to shave off the bark *(left)*. Turn the piece around to debark the other end.

BUILD IT YOURSELF

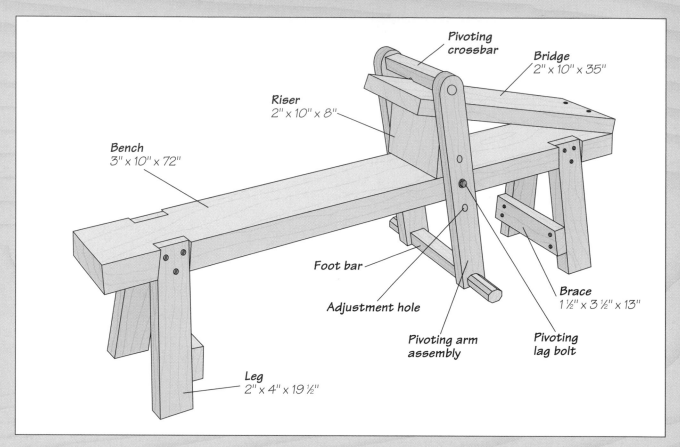

Pivoting crossbar

Bridge
2" x 10" x 35"

Riser
2" x 10" x 8"

Bench
3" x 10" x 72"

Foot bar

Adjustment hole

Brace
1 ½" x 3 ½" x 13"

Pivoting arm assembly

Pivoting lag bolt

Leg
2" x 4" x 19 ½"

A SHAVING HORSE

Also known as a bodger's horse, the shaving horse is the heart of the green woodshop. It is here that stock riven from logs is shaped with drawknives and spokeshaves into legs, rungs, and spindles. Simple to build, the typical shaving horse features a bench, an inclined bridge, and a pivoting arm assembly. By stepping down on the assembly's foot bar, you can lock your workpiece in place between the bridge and the assembly's crossbar. The design of the shaving horse is a marvel of ergonomics; the foot pressure you apply is counterbalanced by the force of pulling the shaving tool toward you.

Shaving horses can be hewn from logs or built with lumber. Any strong, medium-weight wood such as spruce or fir will do. To build the version shown above, start with the bench, which can be hewn from half a log 10 to 12 inches in diameter, or cut to length from rough 3-by-10 lumber. Make the length of the bench to suit your needs; 60 to 72 inches should be sufficient for most shaving work.

Next, cut the legs from rough-sawn 2-by-4 stock slightly longer than you need. The legs are attached to the bench with angled T half-lap joints, reinforced by screws and braces (*right*). To cut the joints, saw notches in the edges

of the bench about 6 inches from the ends to accommodate the legs. Angling the cuts outward and toward the ends

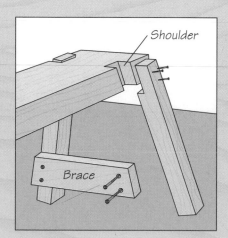

Shoulder

Brace

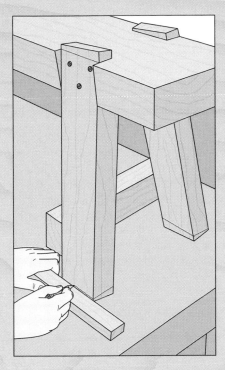

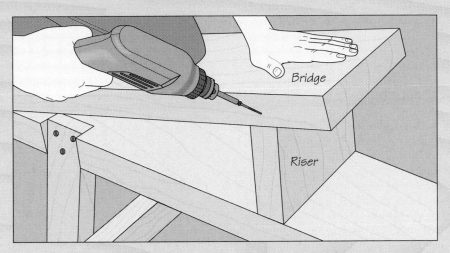

Locate the riser about 30 inches from the back of the bench and screw it in place from underneath. Then screw the bridge to the riser *(above)* and the front of the bridge to the bench.

Next build the pivoting arm. The assembly consists of two arms, a notched crossbar, and a foot bar *(below)*. The crossbar is joined to the arms with through round mortise-and-

tenons, while a bridle joint connects the foot bar to the arms. To determine the length of the arms, first locate the point on the bench where they will be attached. Begin by sitting on the bench and marking a line across the top 4 to 6 inches in front of your knees. Extend the lines down the sides and bore pilot holes on each side of the bench for the lag screws that will hold the arm

will steady the horse. Test-fit each leg in its notch, draw a line on the leg using the notch shoulder as a guide, and cut a matching half-lap in the leg; the shoulder of the half-lap should be ¾ inch deep. Screw the legs in place. Cut the two braces from 2-by-4 stock to fit between the leg's outside edges and screw them to the legs. Now you will need to bevel the bottoms of the legs so that they sit flat and level. With the shaving horse on a flat surface, butt a square board up against all four sides of each leg to mark cutting lines around them *(above)*. Saw the bottoms of the legs flat, then use a flush-cutting saw to cut the tops of the legs flush with the bench.

Next, saw the riser and the bridge to size; the riser should be cut and beveled so that the bridge is inclined at an angle of about 15° to the bench.

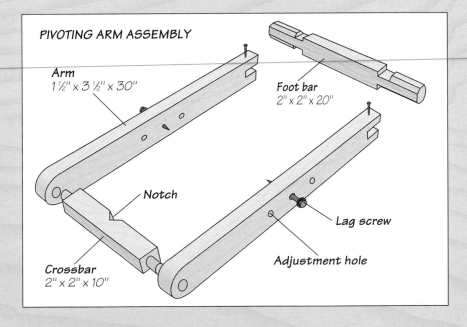

PIVOTING ARM ASSEMBLY

Arm
1 ½" x 3 ½" x 30"

Foot bar
2" x 2" x 20"

Notch

Lag screw

Adjustment hole

Crossbar
2" x 2" x 10"

BUILD IT YOURSELF (continued)

assembly in place. Then place the arm stock vertically against the sides of the bench, centered on this pivot point. At the bottom, the arms will need to clear the ground while the top end must provide at least 3 inches of clearance between the crossbar and the bridge. Once you have determined the required length of the arms, cut them from 2-by-4 stock and bore two countersunk holes through each one for the lag screws. Make additional holes through the arms above and below the first so you will be able to adjust the position of the assembly later to accommodate thicker stock. To prepare the arms for the bars, cut a round mortise through them at the top end and a notch at the bottom.

Next, cut the crossbar to length, making it about 3 inches longer than the width of the bench. Cut round tenons in both ends and a V-shaped notch in the middle of the bottom edge to hold octagonal and circular stock. Set the crossbar aside for now. Next, cut the foot bar, making its length twice that of the crossbar to provide an octagonal-shaped foot rest on each side of the arm assembly. Cut dadoes in the foot bar to match

the notches in the arms, fit the pieces together, and reinforce the joints with screws. With the foot bar attached, slip the arm assembly under the shaving horse and start screwing it in place with the lag screws. Do not tighten the screws all the way immediately; leave them loose enough so you can slip the crossbar in place *(left)*. Do not glue or screw it, but leave the bar free to pivot. Once it is connected to the arms, finish tightening the lag screws.

To use the shaving horse, place the workpiece on the bridge underneath the crossbar. Sitting on the bench, press on the foot bar with both feet to wedge the workpiece in place. You are now ready to shave the stock; always pull the tool toward you *(below)*. To reposition the workpiece, ease the pressure on the foot bar, move the workpiece, and press down on the foot bar again. Once a workpiece becomes circular, place it in the crossbar notch to keep it steady.

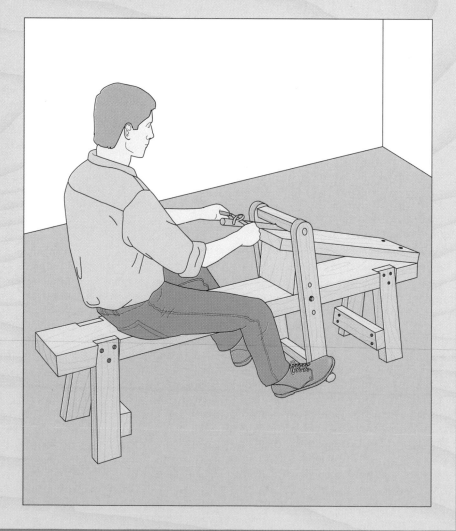

A SLAB-AND-STICK STOOL

Directly descended from primitive benches that were little more than a plank or log supported by three or four sticks, slab-and-stick seating is chair-making at its most basic. Yet the same principles applied in building the simple stool shown below—particularly the interplay of wet and dry wood—are used by Windsor chair makers.

A slab-and-stick stool is an ideal green wood project. The seat can be hewn from a log. The legs and rungs are shaped from green wood blanks, either using a shaving horse or lathe. Woods like oak, ash, or hickory are best if you are drawknifing the legs and rungs; choose maple, birch, cherry, or walnut if you are turning them.

The stool's joinery takes advantage of green wood's hygroscopic, or moisture-absorbing, nature. The dried tenons in the legs absorb moisture from the "wet" seat, causing them to swell and secure the joint.

Some green woodworkers prefer to fashion the seat from 2-inch-thick pine or poplar that has been air-dried to reduce the risk of checking or cracking after assembly. Green wood projects can be left unfinished, but milk paint, boiled linseed oil, or a penetrating oil finish will impart an appropriately rustic look. Stains are rarely used.

The three-legged milking stool is a simple but elegant embodiment of the slab-and-stick style of chair-making. The stool shown above features a saddle seat hewn from poplar, and rungs and legs shaved and turned from ash. The rungs are joined to the legs with standard round mortise-and-tenons. The wedged version of the joint, used to connect the legs to the seat, adds an extra measure of strength and a decorative touch.

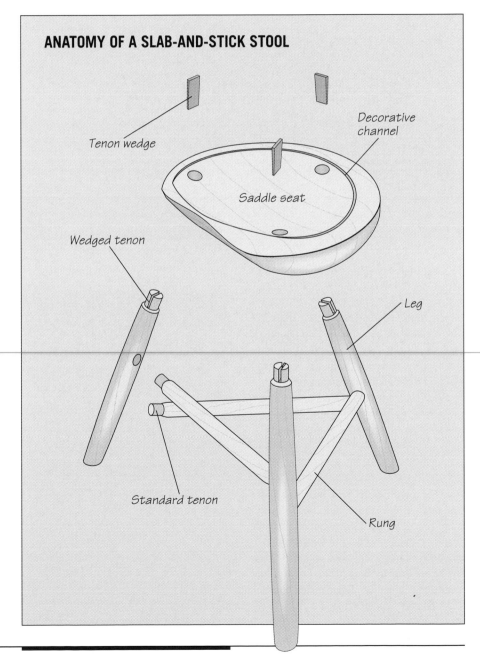

ANATOMY OF A SLAB-AND-STICK STOOL

Tenon wedge

Decorative channel

Saddle seat

Wedged tenon

Leg

Standard tenon

Rung

MAKING THE LEGS AND RUNGS ON THE SHAVING HORSE

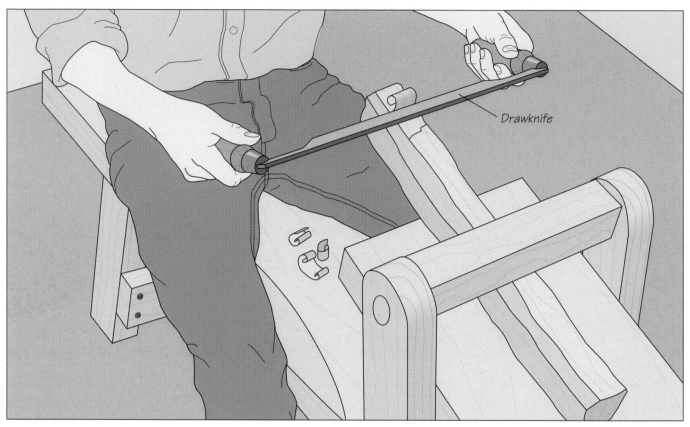

Drawknife

1 Squaring and sizing the blanks
If you are shaving the legs and rungs, you first need to square and size them on the shaving horse, as shown above. The pieces are then shaped into octagons and, finally, cylinders *(step 2)*. The procedure is identical for the legs and rungs, except that the rungs are shaved to a smaller diameter. Use a drawknife to square the blanks. Secure the wood in the shaving horse, with the growth rings visible on the end grain positioned roughly vertically. Holding the drawknife on the blank bevel-side down, pull the tool toward you. The depth of cut depends on how much you tilt the handles; the lower the angle, the shallower the cut. Always follow the wood grain. Once the surface has been squared, turn the blank end-for-end in the horse and shave the other half. Repeat for the other three sides of the blank.

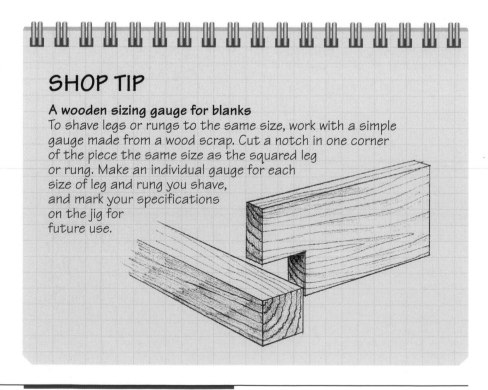

SHOP TIP

A wooden sizing gauge for blanks
To shave legs or rungs to the same size, work with a simple gauge made from a wood scrap. Cut a notch in one corner of the piece the same size as the squared leg or rung. Make an individual gauge for each size of leg and rung you shave, and mark your specifications on the jig for future use.

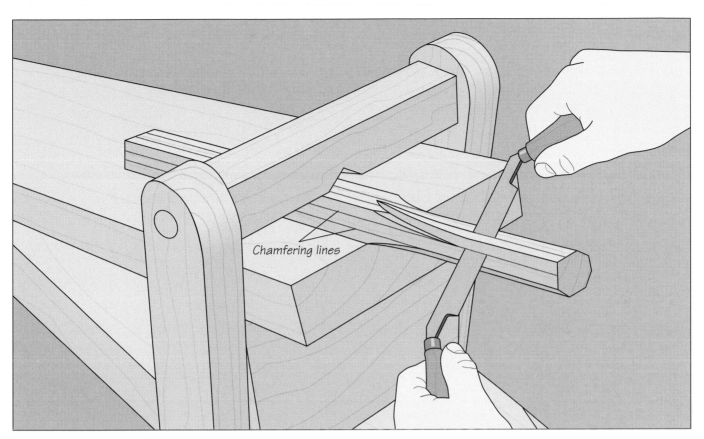

Chamfering lines

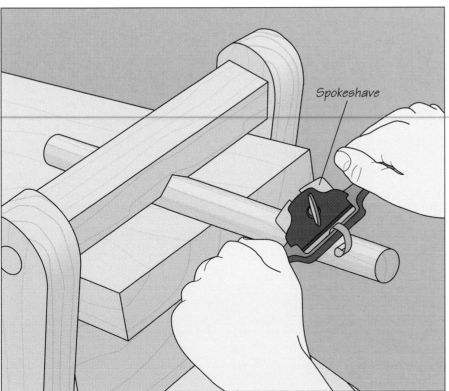

Spokeshave

2 Shaping the legs and rungs

Once you have squared and sized your blanks, cut them into octagons, and then into cylinders. Begin by marking two lines along each surface of a blank to divide it into thirds. Then drawknife the blank into an octagon by chamfering the corners to the marked lines *(above)*. Repeat for the other blanks. Once all the legs and rungs are octagonal secure the blank in the shaving horse crossbar's V-shaped notch and use a spokeshave to round them to the desired diameter *(left)*. Handle the spokeshave as you did the drawknife, always working with the grain and reversing your cutting direction when necessary. Give the legs a slight taper, if you wish.

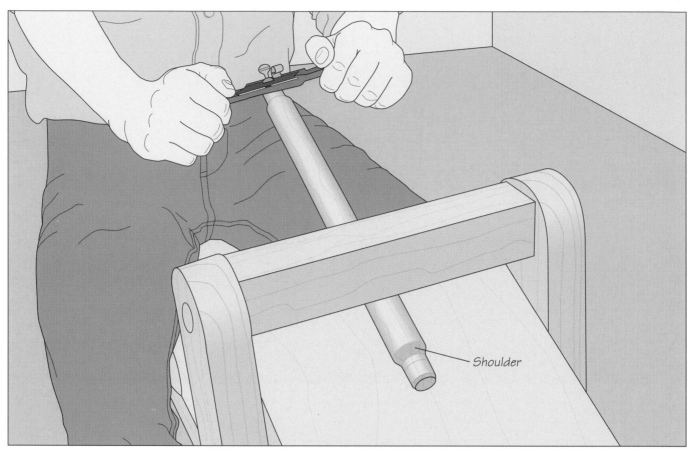

Shoulder

3 Shaving the tenons

Before shaving tenons on both ends of the rungs and the top end of the legs, allow the blanks to air-dry for a week or two. Some woodworkers prefer to dry the ends in hot sand *(page 37)* before shaping the tenons. Once the pieces are ready, prepare a tenon sizing gauge *(right)*. Then, score a shoulder line around the legs and rungs with a shop knife; the tenons should be about 1/16 inch shorter than the mortise depth. Secure the workpiece in the shaving horse and use a spokeshave to shape the tenons as you did the legs and rungs, pulling the tool toward you *(above)*. Periodically test-fit the tenon in its gauge, stopping once the tenon is about 1/32 inch over size. Then sand or file the tenon until it fits tightly in the gauge. Once all the tenons are shaped, use the knife to chamfer each end; this will make them easier to drive into the mortises.

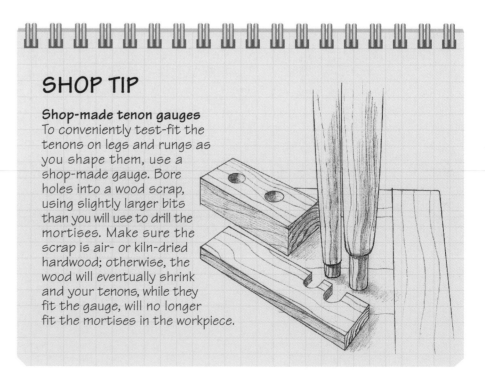

SHOP TIP

Shop-made tenon gauges
To conveniently test-fit the tenons on legs and rungs as you shape them, use a shop-made gauge. Bore holes into a wood scrap, using slightly larger bits than you will use to drill the mortises. Make sure the scrap is air- or kiln-dried hardwood; otherwise, the wood will eventually shrink and your tenons, while they fit the gauge, will no longer fit the mortises in the workpiece.

TURNING THE LEGS AND RUNGS

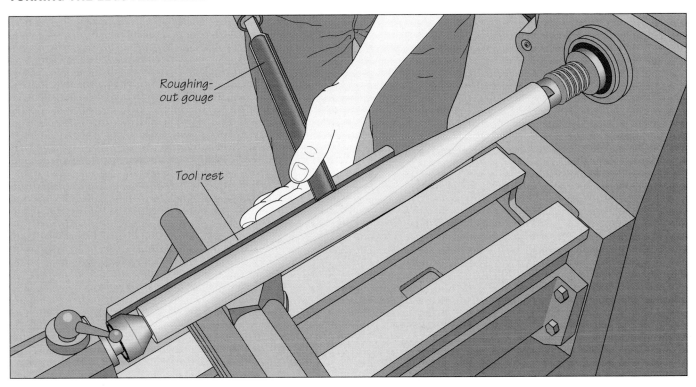

Roughing-out gouge

Tool rest

1 Turning the legs
Some woodworkers prefer to turn legs and rungs on a lathe. Mount a blank on the machine and adjust the tool rest as close to the workpiece as possible without touching it. Use a roughing-out gouge to turn the blank into a cylinder; supporting the blade with one hand, prop it against the tool rest so that the bevel rubs against the stock as the cutting edge slices into it *(above)*. Working from side to side, turn the blank until the cylinder has the proper diameter. Taper the lower half of the leg, if desired.

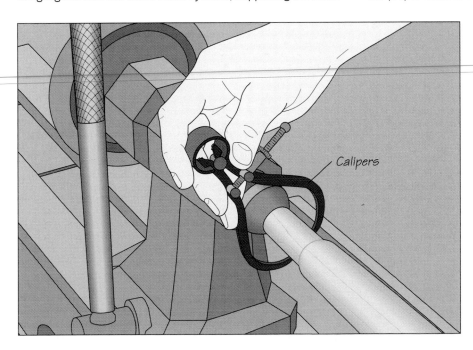

Calipers

2 Turning the tenons
Use a gouge or skew chisel to turn tenons on both ends of the rungs and at the top end of the legs. Periodically turn off the lathe and check the diameter of each tenon with a pair of calipers set to the appropriate diameter *(left)*. Since you are working with green wood, turn the tenons slightly larger than needed, let them air-dry or use hot sand *(page 37)*, then bring them to their finished diameter.

MAKING THE SEAT

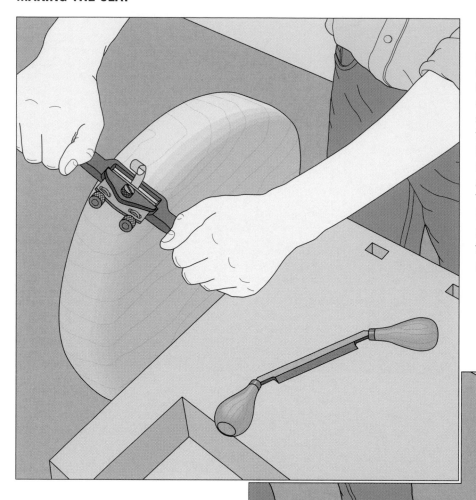

Hand adze

1 **Rounding over the blank**
The seat blank can either be split from a log, or made from air-dried stock. If you are splitting your blank, avoid the pith, or center, of the log, as this wood is of poor quality. Chop the blank as square as possible with a hewing hatchet, then outline the seat's circular shape on the top of the blank with a waterproof pencil. Clamp the blank in a vise and cut it using a bowsaw, as shown in the color photo on page 14. The first steps in shaping the seat are smoothing its circumference and rounding over its underside with a drawknife. Then, switch to a spokeshave to smooth the contours *(left)*, always following the grain.

2 **Dishing out the seat**
Once the circumference of the seat has been shaped, mark out the sitting area, or saddle, and rough out the waste using a hand adze. Wearing steel-toed boots, step on the edges of the blank to hold it steady and chop out the saddle from both sides toward the middle *(right)*. Try to cut with the wood grain, using short strokes. Make sure your feet are not in line with your stroke.

3 Smoothing the saddle

Secure the seat between two bench dogs on your workbench; use wood pads to protect the edges. Start with an inshave to smooth the rough surface left by the adze. Working from the edges of the saddle toward the middle, hold the inshave with both hands and pull it toward you; always follow the grain *(right, top)*. You can further smooth the saddle with a carver's hook, scraper, or scorp *(right, bottom)*. Use a hand plane to smooth the flat surface of the seat, and a drawknife and spokeshave to gently slope its front edge down to meet the bevel. Sand the seat with coarse sandpaper, leaving the final sanding for when you have assembled the seat and legs *(page 39)*.

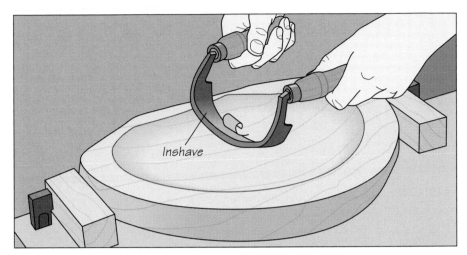

Inshave

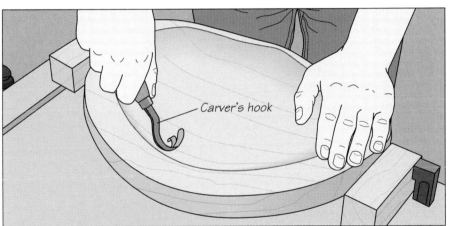

Carver's hook

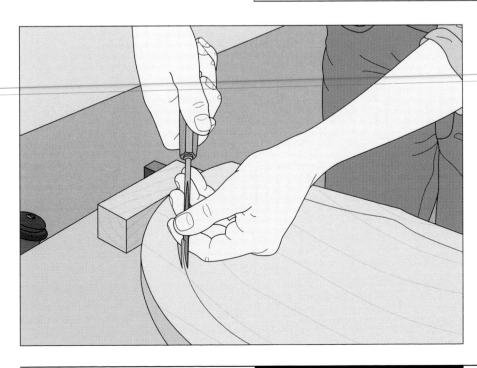

4 Carving the channel

Use a ¼-inch veiner *(page 73)* to carve the channel that separates the hollowed-out saddle from the flattened back of the seat *(left)*. This decorative groove serves to sharpen the transition between the saddle and the flat part of the seat.

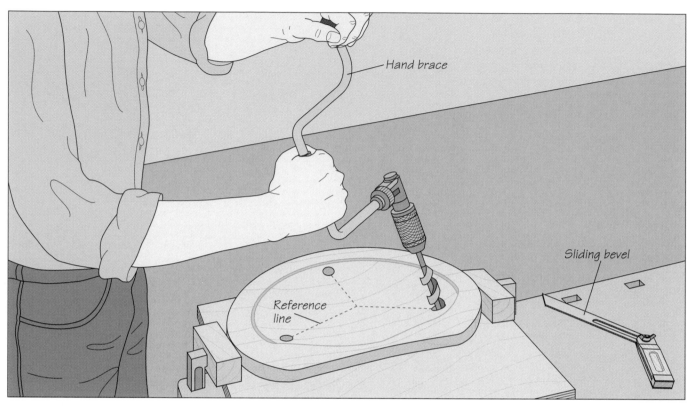

Hand brace

Sliding bevel

Reference line

5 Boring the mortises for the legs

Drill the leg mortises through the seat with a hand brace fitted with an auger bit. Since the stool is supported by three legs, you need to bore angled holes for them so that the legs will be splayed out at an angle of about 30° from the vertical; use a protractor to set a sliding bevel to this angle to help you guide your brace. Mark the center of the seat and the three holes, then draw reference lines between the hole marks and the center. Clamp the seat face-up to a work surface. To drill each mortise, hold the tool at a 30° angle and align it with the appropriate reference line. Bore the hole *(above)* until the bit's lead screw breaks through the bottom of the seat, then turn the seat over and finish drilling the mortises from the bottom.

SHOP TIP

A guide for boring angled mortises
As an alternative to relying on a bevel square to guide angled drilling operations, use a shop-made guide from a piece of plywood. When the desired angle is cut on one end of the guide, set the piece on edge alongside your hand brace. Align the bit with the cut end as you begin to bore your holes.

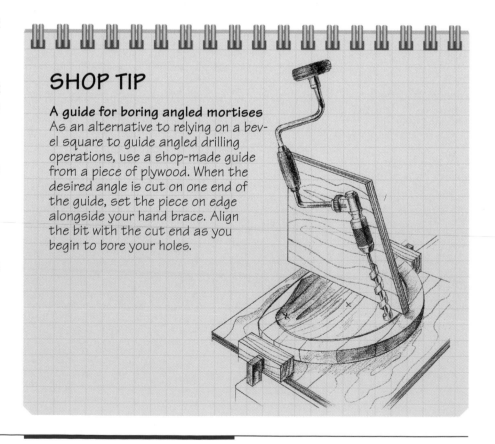

ASSEMBLING THE SEAT AND LEGS

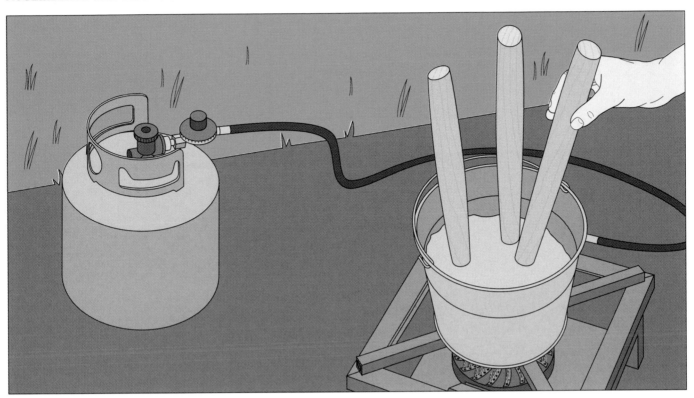

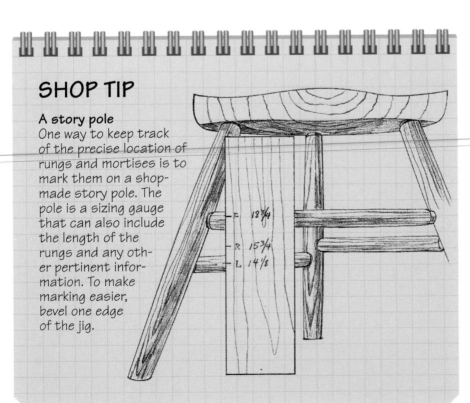

SHOP TIP

A story pole
One way to keep track of the precise location of rungs and mortises is to mark them on a shopmade story pole. The pole is a sizing gauge that can also include the length of the rungs and any other pertinent information. To make marking easier, bevel one edge of the jig.

F 18¾
R 15¾
L 14⅛

1 Drying the tenons
The leg and rung tenons can be dried either after or before they are sized *(page 32)*. In both cases, you can do the job with hot sand. This will remove virtually all the moisture from the tenons, which will then absorb moisture from the mortises and swell when the stool is assembled; at the same time, the seat will shrink around the tenons as it dries, locking the joints together. Working outdoors, heat a bucket of fine, dry sand with a propane-fired cooker. Insert the legs and rungs into the bucket so only the tenons are buried in the sand. Use a thermometer to monitor the temperature regularly, and adjust the flame to keep the sand between 140° and 160° F. The wood will be charred quickly if subjected to higher temperatures. Leave the tenons in the hot sand for a few hours, rotating them regularly to avoid scorching *(above)*.

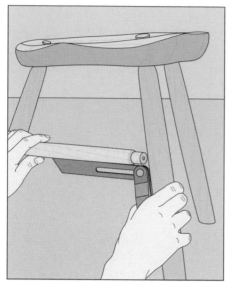

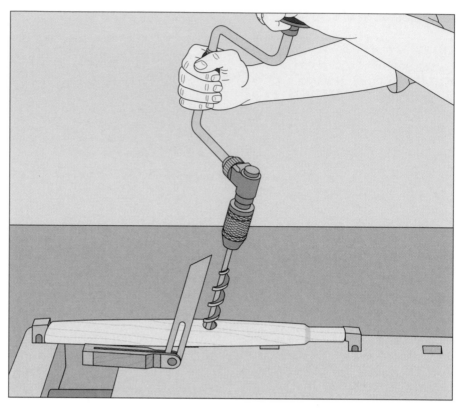

2 Boring the mortises for the rungs

Dry assemble the legs in the seat, positioning the legs to expose the most attractive grain pattern. Then hold one rung in position between two legs, and mark its location. Also measure the angle between the rung and the leg with a sliding bevel *(above, left)*. Repeat for the other rungs. The rungs should be offset from each other so their mortises are horizontal but not all at the same level. To keep the tenons from absorbing moisture from the seat and swelling before final assembly, remove the legs from the chair once you are finished measuring. For each mortise, secure the rung on a work surface and bore the hole with a hand brace and auger bit, using the sliding bevel as a guide *(above, right)*.

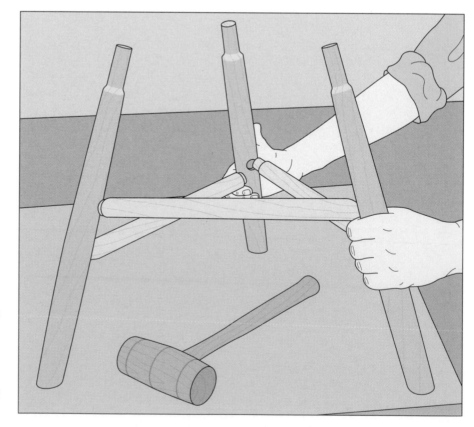

3 Assembling the stool

Once you have bored all the mortises, assemble the legs and rungs *(right)*. The tenons should fit tightly enough for you to need a mallet to tap them in. Fit the seat onto the leg tenons and tap it into place. Although the parts need not be glued together, you can reinforce the joints with either white or hide glue.

4 Tapping in the tenon wedges

The leg tenons in the seat are wedged, tightening the joint further and ensuring that the tenons will not loosen if the seat shrinks as a result of drying. Kerf the tenons by striking a firmer chisel with a mallet; to avoid splitting the seat, orient the slots so that they are perpendicular to the grain of the seat. Then cut hardwood wedges to fit into the slots; make them the same width as the tenon, but a few inches longer, and no thicker than ¼ inch at the broad end. Drive the wedges into the slots as far as they can go with a mallet *(right)*. Use a flush-cutting saw or dovetail saw to trim the wedges even with the end of the tenon.

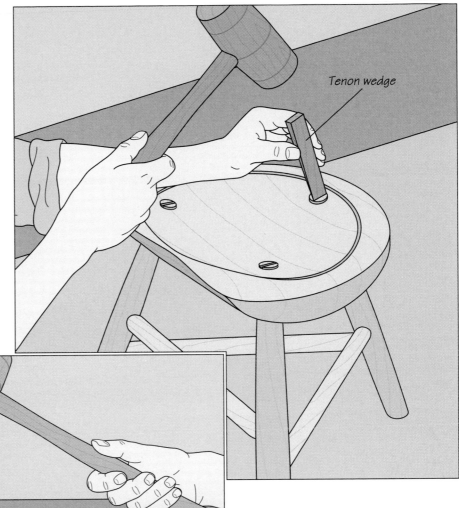

Tenon wedge

Gouge

5 Finishing off the stool

Trim the tenons flush with the surface of the seat with a wide, shallow carving gouge; use a mallet to strike the gouge *(left)*. To avoid tearout, cut halfway through each tenon, then chop out the remaining excess from the other side. To finish the legs, cut their bottoms so the seat will rest level. Follow the same technique used to level the shaving horse legs *(page 27)*. Finally, sand all the surfaces of the stool smooth, and air-dry the piece for several weeks before finishing it.

BENDING WOOD

Steam bending can make even the densest of hardwoods pliable; the blistered big-leaf maple living room table shown above, built by Toronto cabinetmaker Michael Fortune, features a curved, black center panel which was steam-bent from cherry.

At first glance, the idea of bending wood appears to contradict all that woodworkers have learned about their craft and the need for precise measurement and stock that is straight, square, and even. Yet when it comes to reproducing the classic curves of a Windsor chair, a Shaker box, or a rounded blanket box lid, a straight piece of wood will not fit the bill. Nature is no help either; few tree trunks grow the curves that function well and please the eye. Instead, woodworkers have devised ingenious ways of bending wood to suit their needs.

The chapter that follows is an introduction to the craft. Once you understand why wood can bend, and which species bend best *(page 42)*, you will be able to use the techniques shown here to produce such items as the continuous arm of a Windsor chair *(page 51)*, a Shaker box *(page 54)*, or a coopered blanket box lid *(page 67)*.

Wood can be bent either dry or wet. The bending techniques for each are different. When wood is air dried to a moisture content suitable for cabinetry it will bend if it is resawn into thin strips and glued up as a curved laminate *(page 57)*. Another option for dry stock is to kerf it repeatedly and then bend it, as shown on page 61.

Wet wood—stock with a high moisture content—bends more readily than dry wood. Woodworkers who harvest their own timber or work with green wood know that thin strips of freshly cut wood are pliable. And, if the wood is clamped until it dries, it will retain its bent shape. Steam bending utilizes this principle to flex wood in a controlled fashion. By exposing wood to heat and saturated water vapor, the fibers of the wood can be softened to the point where tight curves can be produced without splitting the wood.

Bending is typically done with the help of a steam box *(page 45)*, or with some plastic ABS pipe. Following the instructions provided on page 46, you can build a durable and effective shop-made steamer. Once the wood is steamed, the blank is bent over plywood forms shaped to the desired curve, then clamped and strapped in place until it dries. As simple as it sounds, steam bending is not completely predictable. Just as no two trees are identical, no two bends will produce exactly the same results. Be prepared to proceed by trial and error.

Made from quartersawn veneers, the cherry Shaker boxes shown at left demonstrate how moisture—in this case hot water—can be used to soften wood fibers, allowing the sheets to be bent around a form.

CHOOSING WOOD

By nature, wood is an elastic material. Trees must move with the wind, and the complex design of their cellular structure makes this possible, even long after a tree has been felled. The key to bending wood lies in the natural polymer called lignin that bonds wood cells together. Steaming the wood softens the lignin bond, allowing the wood to be bent into a new shape. Wood will stretch very little before fracturing, but will compress to a tremendous degree.

Not all woods bend the same. Just how far you can bend a piece of wood depends on its grain and figure. Most readily available domestic air-dried hardwoods will bend to moderate curves; curves as tight as 1 inch in radius can be achieved with species such as ash, white oak, and elm. (Because of their different cellular structure, softwoods are poorly suited for steam bending.) Some exotic woods are difficult to bend; their dense, interlocked grain often collapses during bending. For an indication of what woods are best for steam and laminate bending, see the chart on the opposite page.

The moisture content of wood is critical to its bendability. The more a wood's cells are saturated with moisture, the more easily it can be bent. Air-dried wood with a moisture content of 25 percent to 35 percent is superior to kiln-dried stock. Green wood, or wood hewn from a log, is good—unless it contains free moisture that will cause cell rupture in a sharp bend. There are two kinds of steam bending: supported and unsupported. Unsupported steam bending *(page 51)*, in which no tension strap is used, can only be done with green wood. It produces less consistent results than supported steam bending *(pages 47 and 50)*, which uses air-dried wood and a tension strap with end stops.

Successful bends start with straight-grained boards free of decay, shakes, knots, surface checks, pith, and other defects. Wood riven from a log is ideal, as the cuts follow the wood fibers rather than shearing them.

When wood is bent unsupported, compression occurs on the inside of a bend, while tension is exerted on the outside. Steaming wood enhances its ability to be compressed, yet does little to prevent tension failure, as shown by the split workpiece (left, top). By using a tension strap with end stops (page 47) to support the workpiece along its convex edge during bending, most of the tension is deflected to the concave edge as compression; the result is the strong, unbroken, and stable curve illustrated (left, bottom).

WHY BEND WOOD?

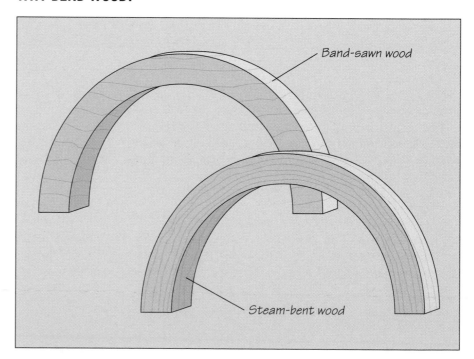

Band-sawn wood

Steam-bent wood

Following the grain

Virtually any curve can be band-sawn in a piece of wood. But this method has its drawbacks: Besides wasting a good deal of raw material, the cutting will invariably involve some sawing across the grain *(above, top)*. This results in weak short grain either around the curve or at the ends, and a considerable reduction in the strength of the bend. Bending wood not only results in less waste, but it also reorients the wood's fibers along the axis of the curve *(above, bottom)*. This results in uniform long grain along the curve, producing a bend that will be much more resistant to failure.

SUITABILITY OF VARIOUS AIR-DRIED WOOD SPECIES FOR STEAM BENDING

GOOD

(Can be steam-bent to a tight curve with radius of less than 5 inches; based on 1-inch-thick stock supported by a tension strap)

- Ash, white *(Fraxinus americana)*
- Beech *(Fagus spp.)*
- Elm, Dutch *(Ulmus hollandica)*
- Elm, rock *(Ulmus thomasii)*
- Elm, white *(Ulmus americana)*
- Hackberry *(Celtis occidentalis)*
- Hickory *(Carya spp.)*
- Oak, red *(Quercus rubra)*
- Oak, white *(Quercus spp.)*
- Pecan *(Carya spp.)*
- Sycamore *(Platanus occidentalis)*
- Walnut *(Juglans spp.)*

FAIR

(Can be steam-bent to a moderate curve limited to radius between 5 and 10 inches; based on 1-inch-thick stock supported by a tension strap)

- Birch *(Betula spp.)*
- Cherry *(Prunus avium)*
- Chestnut *(Castanea spp.)*
- Gum, red *(Liquidambar styraciflua)*
- Maple, hard *(Acer saccharum)*
- Mulberry *(Morus lactea)*

DIFFICULT

(Can only be steam-bent to a large radius, gentle curve; based on 1-inch-thick stock supported by a tension strap)

- Alder *(Alnus glutinosa)*
- Butternut *(Juglans cinerea)*
- Cedar, western red *(Thuja plicata)*
- Douglas-fir *(Pseudotsuga menziesii)*
- Hemlock *(Tsuga heterophylla)*
- Mahogany, African *(Khaya spp.)*
- Poplar, yellow *(Liriodendron tulipfera)*
- Willow *(Salix nigra)*

SUITABILITY OF VARIOUS WOOD SPECIES FOR LAMINATE BENDING

GOOD

(Can be bent to a tight curve with radius of less than 5 inches; based on thin laminations of ⅛-inch-thick veneers)

- Ash, white *(Fraxinus americana)*
- Ash, European *(Fraxinus excelsior)*
- Beech *(Fagus spp.)*
- Elm, Dutch *(Ulmus hollandica)*
- Elm, rock *(Ulmus thomasii)*
- Oak, red *(Quercus rubra)*
- Walnut *(Juglans spp.)*

FAIR

(Can be bent to a moderate curve limited to radius greater than 5 inches; based on thin laminations of ⅛-inch-thick veneers)

- Cherry *(Prunus spp.)*
- Ebony *(Diospyros crassiflora)*
- Elm, English *(Carya spp.)*
- Hickory *(Carya spp.)*
- Oak, white *(Quercus spp.)*
- Sycamore *(Platanus occidentalis)*
- Teak *(Tectona grandis)*
- Walnut, African *(Lovoa trichilioides)*
- Yew *(Taxus baccata)*

DIFFICULT

(Can be bent to a moderate curve with a radius greater than 10 inches; based on thin laminations of ⅛-inch-thick veneers)

- Avodiré *(Turreanthus africanus)*
- Cedar, western red *(Thuja plicata)*
- Douglas-fir *(Pseudotsuga menziesii)*
- Mahogany, African *(Khaya spp.)*
- Spruce, sitka *(Picea sitchensis)*

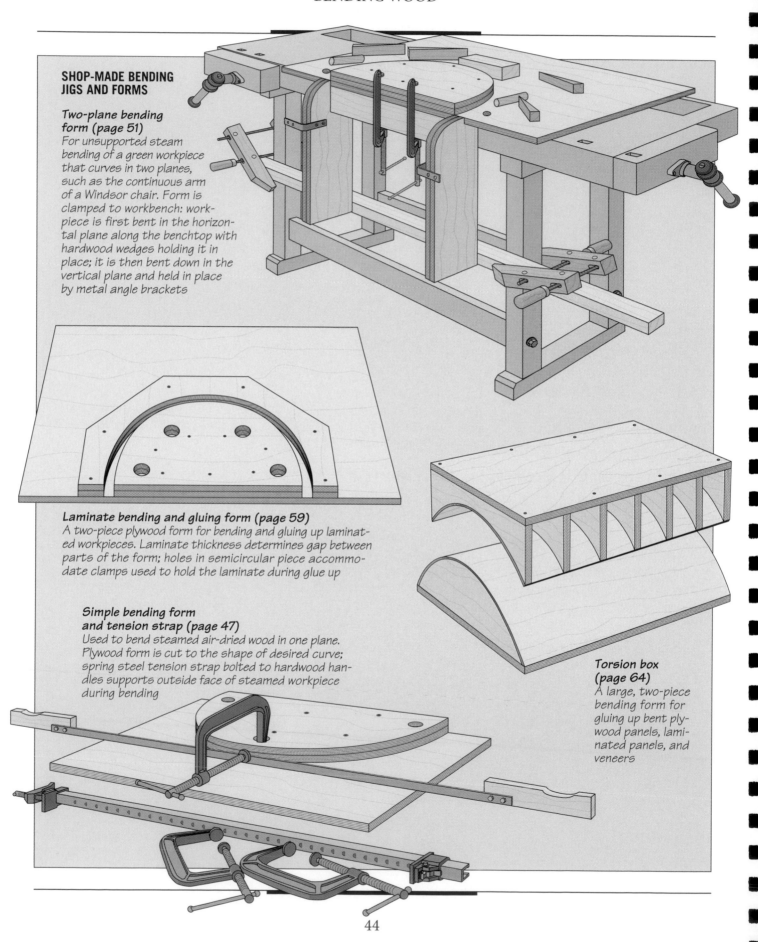

SHOP-MADE BENDING JIGS AND FORMS

Two-plane bending form (page 51)
For unsupported steam bending of a green workpiece that curves in two planes, such as the continuous arm of a Windsor chair. Form is clamped to workbench; workpiece is first bent in the horizontal plane along the benchtop with hardwood wedges holding it in place; it is then bent down in the vertical plane and held in place by metal angle brackets

Laminate bending and gluing form (page 59)
A two-piece plywood form for bending and gluing up laminated workpieces. Laminate thickness determines gap between parts of the form; holes in semicircular piece accommodate clamps used to hold the laminate during glue up

Simple bending form and tension strap (page 47)
Used to bend steamed air-dried wood in one plane. Plywood form is cut to the shape of desired curve; spring steel tension strap bolted to hardwood handles supports outside face of steamed workpiece during bending

Torsion box (page 64)
A large, two-piece bending form for gluing up bent plywood panels, laminated panels, and veneers

STEAM BENDING

The two essential elements of any wood-steaming setup are a steam generator and an enclosed steamer box to hold the wood. The box can be simple. The version shown below is made of ¾-inch exterior-grade plywood, assembled with rabbet-and-dado joints. Any tight-fitting joinery method will do. The steamer shown in the photo at right and described on page 46 is shop-made from ABS pipe. Whichever design you choose, be sure to make the steamer longer than the pieces to be bent, and seal it tightly to keep the steam from escaping. Also, include a small drain hole at one end and place the steamer on a slight incline to allow the condensed steam to run out. If you are using a gas-powered steam source, it is safest to do your steaming outside; local fire codes may insist on it. You can bend wood indoors using an electric wallpaper steamer *(page 49)* or

even a kettle, but remember that a considerable amount of water vapor will be produced.

There are no simple rules for the length of time wood must be steamed before it is sufficiently pliable. As a rough guide, steam air-dried lumber for one hour per inch of thickness; half that time is adequate for green wood. Once steamed, the workpiece is bent around a form using a tension strap *(page 47)* on the outside of the stock. Not only will the strap allow you to bend tighter curves; it will also ensure that the wood does not split on the outer face of the bend.

After bending, tie the ends of the workpiece together with cord and let it dry. During drying, the lignin bond that was softened during heating will reform as the wood cools. After approximately one week, a bent piece of 1-by-3 stock will be dry.

Made from ABS pipe and fittings, the steam bender shown above is hooked up to a water can and a propane-fired cooker. The workpiece is inserted at one end of the pipe and the steam enters through a coupling located at its middle, allowing for uniform distribution of the steam around the workpiece.

ANATOMY OF A STEAM BOX

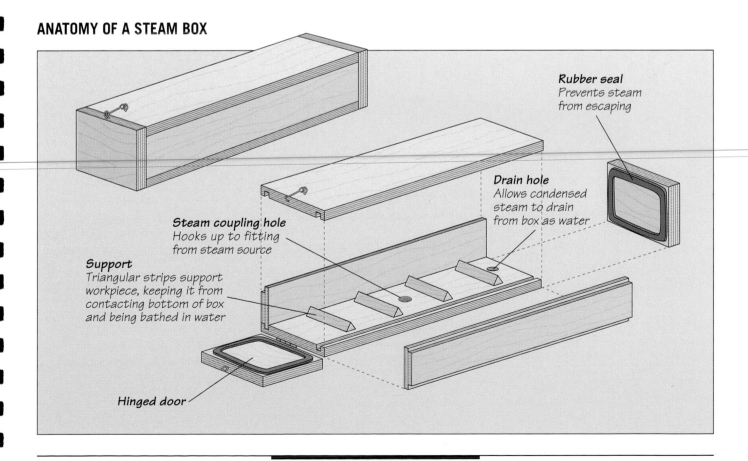

Rubber seal
Prevents steam from escaping

Drain hole
Allows condensed steam to drain from box as water

Steam coupling hole
Hooks up to fitting from steam source

Support
Triangular strips support workpiece, keeping it from contacting bottom of box and being bathed in water

Hinged door

BUILD IT YOURSELF

A SHOP-MADE PIPE STEAMER

An economical and durable wood steamer like the one shown below can be fashioned from 2-by-4s and 4-inch-diameter ABS pipe and fittings. The device features support racks inside the pipe and a removable cap at each end for easy access. The steam source is a water can connected to the steamer by a length of plastic hose; the water in the can is heated by a propane-fired cooker. (This setup should only be used outdoors.) The steam source should have a removable, screw-type cap.

To build the steamer, start with a length of Schedule 80 ABS pipe longer than the piece of wood you wish to bend. Cut it in half and bored a series of holes through both pieces to accommodate ⅜-inch zinc-coated machine bolts and nuts as shown. These bolts

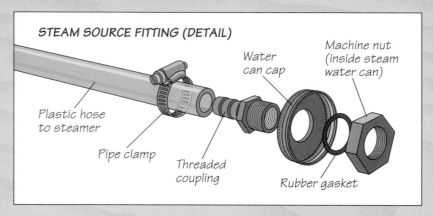

STEAM SOURCE FITTING (DETAIL)

Plastic hose to steamer

Pipe clamp

Threaded coupling

Water can cap

Machine nut (inside steam water can)

Rubber gasket

will support wood inside the steamer to prevent it from lying in condensed water. (The zinc coating will prevent the bolts from staining the wood.) Bore the holes below the centerline of the pipe to provide room for the wood. Install the bolts, using both steel and rubber washers on both sides to make

an airtight seal. Now glue both halves of the pipe to an ABS T connector. Bore a ½-inch drain hole at one end to release moisture and prevent excess pressure. Then glue a connector pipe cut from 1½-inch ABS pipe to the spout of the T connector. Next, cut a length of plastic hose that will connect the steamer to the water can; the fittings required for the water can end are shown in the inset. (The fittings for the steamer end of the hose are identical, except that an ABS end cap is used instead of the water can cap; the end cap is glued and screwed to the connector pipe.) Make sure the fittings are airtight. Lastly, build a 2-by-4 frame to support the steamer. Nail a small support block at one end so the steamer will rest on a slight incline and the excess water will run out of the drain hole.

To use the steamer, carefully connect the gas cooker to a propane tank. Fill the water can, seal it tightly, and set it on the cooker. Secure the removable end caps on the steamer, light the cooker, and let the steamer build up steam. **(Caution: Do not let the steamer or steam source become pressurized.)** Then follow Step 3 on page 48.

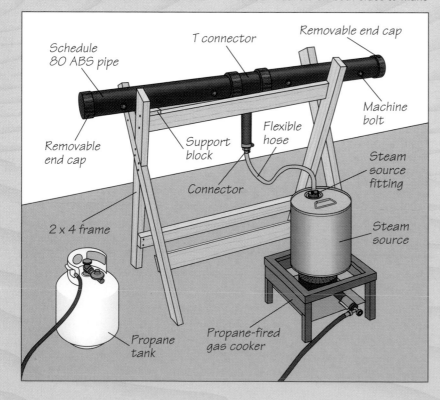

Schedule 80 ABS pipe

T connector

Removable end cap

Removable end cap

Support block

Connector

Flexible hose

Machine bolt

Steam source fitting

2 x 4 frame

Steam source

Propane tank

Propane-fired gas cooker

SUPPORTED STEAM BENDING

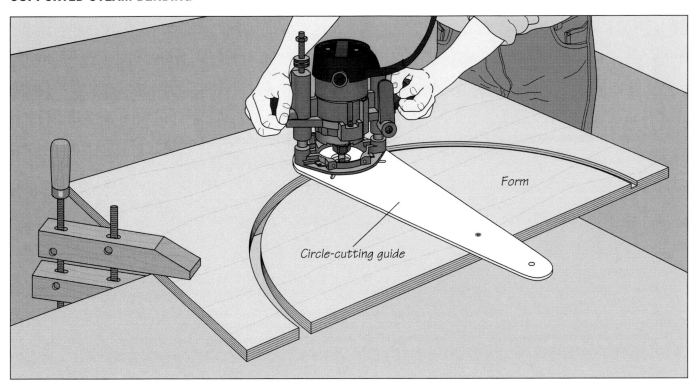

Form

Circle-cutting guide

1 Making the form
To bend steamed wood in a single plane, such as a simple U-shaped arc, build a bending form from 2 sheets of ¾-inch plywood. The form shown on page 48 will handle stock up to ¾ inch thick; to bend thicker wood, try the bending table shown on page 50. Mark the radius you want on the plywood and cut the form using a router fitted with a straight bit and a circle-cutting guide. Make the cut in two passes, increasing the depth of cut for the second pass *(above)*. Prepare a second piece of plywood the same way as the first and screw the two pieces together. Bore three or four evenly spaced holes near the outside circumference of the form to hold C clamps as shown on page 49. Sand the outside edge of the form. Mount the form on a ¾-inch plywood base, and mark the center of the bend on the form.

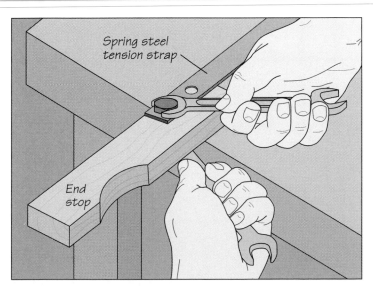

Spring steel
tension strap

End
stop

2 Making the tension strap
To support the wood during the bending process, you will need a spring steel tension strap. It must be at least as wide as the stock being bent, and should be mounted with end stops large enough to cover the ends of the workpiece. Have a metalworking shop cut the strap from ¹⁄₁₆-inch spring steel a few inches longer than your workpiece. Also have holes drilled through the strap at each end to affix the end stops; the distance between the stops should equal the length of the workpiece. If you will be bending a species like oak that is likely to be stained by steel, line the facing side of the strap with a strip of aluminum foil or plastic sheeting. Mark the center of the strap and bolt on the end stops *(left)*.

3 Steaming the wood

Fire up your steam source and mark the center of the workpiece to be bent. Once steam begins to come out of the steamer's drain hole, place the workpiece inside. Close the steamer's drain hole tightly and let the wood sit until it is softened. To avoid scalding your hands when removing the wood from the steamer, wear work gloves and use tongs *(right)*.

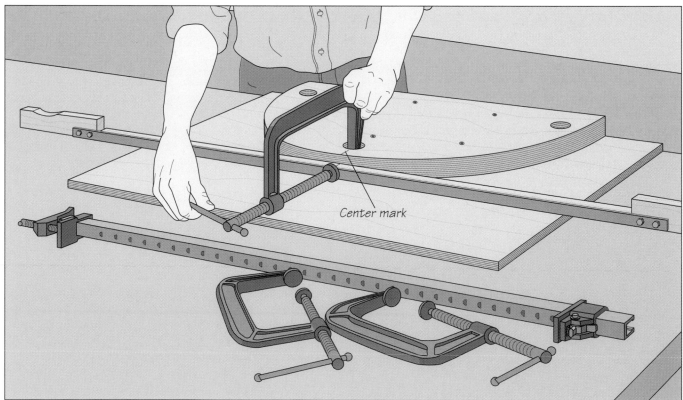

Center mark

4 Clamping the middle of the bend

As soon as the wood is out of the steamer, place it on the bending form. Aligning the center marks on the tension strap, the workpiece, and the form, secure the three together with a C clamp *(above)*. Work quickly to complete steps 4 and 5 in as little time as possible; within 45 to 60 seconds of leaving the steamer, the wood will begin to cool enough to make it unbendable.

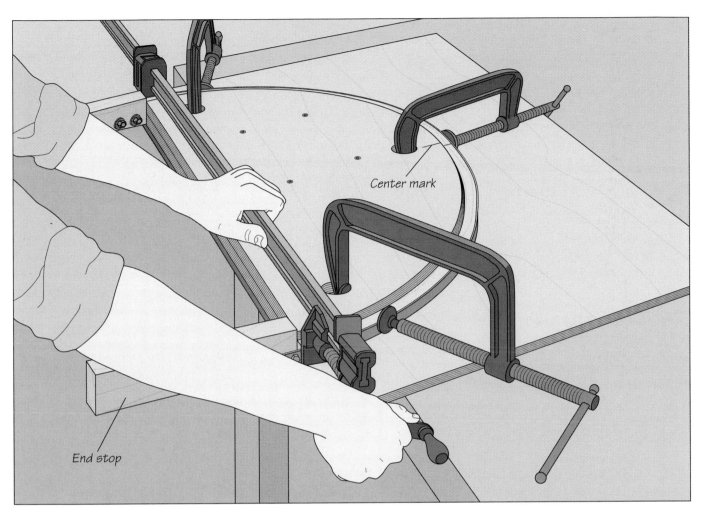

Center mark

End stop

5 Clamping the sides
Firmly and steadily pull one of the end stops toward the form. As soon as the workpiece contacts the form near the clamp hole, secure it in place with a C clamp. (You may need to work with a helper.) Repeat on the other side of the form and clamp the other half of the workpiece in place. Next, secure the ends of the workpiece to the form with a bar clamp *(above)*. Let the wood dry on the form until it is cool to the touch—about 30 minutes—then remove it, secure its ends together with cord, and allow another week of drying time.

SHOP TIP

An alternate source of steam
While propane-fired cookers are often used to heat water as a steam source for bending wood, a safe and clean alternative is a rented electric wallpaper steamer. Most models can generate a full head of steam in under 45 minutes, and provide continuous steam for more than an hour. Most units have fittings that can be directly connected to your steamer.

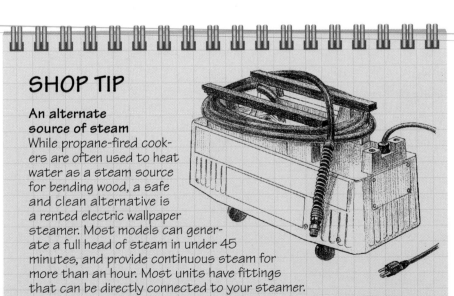

BUILD IT YOURSELF

A BENDING TABLE

The considerable force required to bend pieces of steamed wood more than ¾ inch thick calls for a stronger and more adaptable clamping arrangement than a simple benchtop form and tension strap. The shop-made bending table shown below is made of four sheets of plywood laminated together, and features a grid of holes that can accommodate a variety of custom-made bending forms. The forms, as well as any end stops or wedges that are needed, are held in place by locating pins bolted through the form and table. Cut from the same type of iron pipe used to make pipe clamps, the pins are designed to withstand the immense shear forces of the bending process.

To make the table, start with the top, cutting four sheets of ¾-inch plywood to the desired size and gluing them together. Then drill a grid of ⅞-inch holes at 4-inch intervals through the top. Use the same bit to drill holes through any forms you will be using, ensuring that their spacing matches that of the holes in the tabletop. Complete the table by attaching legs to the top. To make the locating pins *(inset)*, cut short lengths of ½-inch-inside-diameter iron pipe, and weld large washers to the top of each to facilitate easy insertion and removal. The pins should be as long as the combined thicknesses of the form and tabletop. Make a tension strap *(page 47)* slightly wider than the

thickness of the workpiece and attach end stops to the strap with hex bolts and washers; the distance between the stops should be the same as the length of the workpiece.

To use the bending table, position the form on the top, aligning its holes with those in the table. Slip a locating pin into each hole in the form and the corresponding hole in the table, securing the form in place. Bend the workpiece as you would on a benchtop form *(page 48)*. When bending thick pieces of wood, it is helpful to reinforce the tension straps by bolting hardwood blocks to the outside of the strap. These pieces help prevent the wood from twisting out of plane as it is bent.

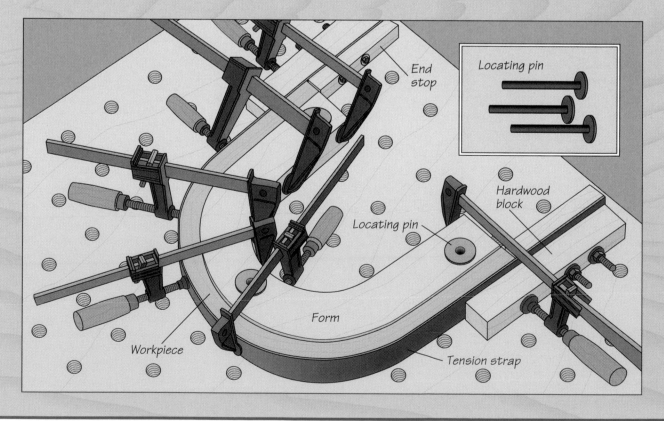

End stop

Locating pin

Hardwood block

Locating pin

Form

Workpiece

Tension strap

TWO-PLANE BENDING

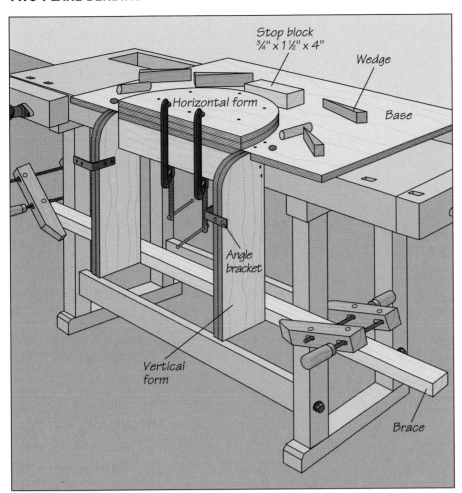

Stop block
¾" x 1½" x 4"

Wedge

Base

Horizontal form

Angle
bracket

Vertical
form

Brace

1 Building a two-plane bending form
A two-plane bending form is needed to bend green wood in more than one plane (when making Windsor chair arms, for example). The model illustrated is made from ¾-inch plywood and is designed to be clamped to a workbench. The horizontal form is similar to a single-plane bending form *(page 47)*, except it uses a hardwood stop block and two dowels positioned around the form to secure the work. Screw the block to the base from underneath; bore two holes into the base for the dowels. The space between the blocks and dowels and the form should equal the thickness of the workpiece and the wedges used to secure it in place. Make the two vertical forms as you would the horizontal one; their radius should equal the desired curvature. Notch the top edge of the vertical forms and screw them to the base; position the forms to be in line with the workpiece when it is clamped to the horizontal form. Screw a metal angle bracket to each vertical form—projecting a bit more than workpiece's thickness—to hold the wood in place. Lastly, clamp a brace between the workbench legs and the vertical forms to resist the inward pressure during bending.

2 Wedging the middle of the bend
Because this form does not include a tension strap, the workpiece to be bent should be green and no thicker than ¾ inch. Determine the transition point where the wood will bend vertically, and use a drawknife to reduce the thickness of the piece slightly. Once the wood has been sufficiently steamed *(page 48)*, remove it from the steamer and place it on the bending form. Align the center marks on the workpiece and form, and clamp the workpiece to the middle of the form by tapping wedges in place *(right)*. Work quickly, completing steps 2 through 4 as soon as possible.

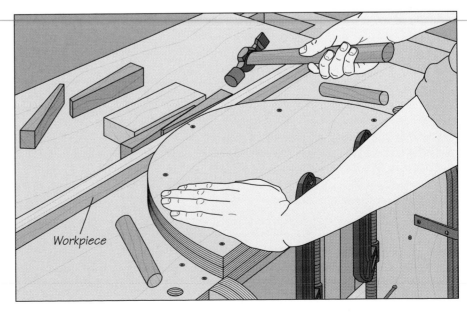

Workpiece

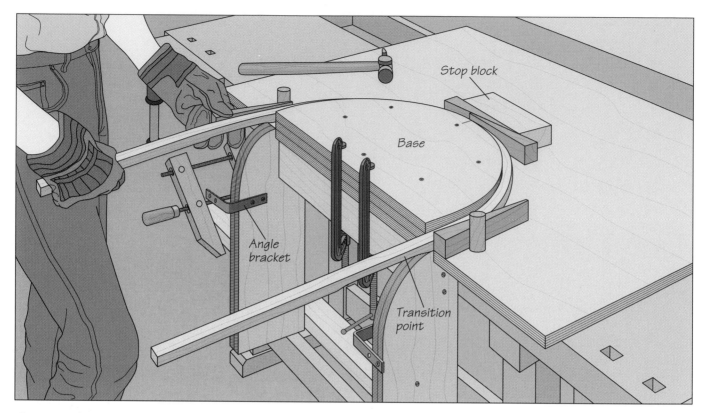

3 Wedging the sides of the workpiece

Pull one end of the workpiece toward the horizontal form firmly and steadily until it contacts the side of the form. Working with a helper, if necessary, position a wedge alongside the workpiece and insert a dowel into the hole in the base to secure the workpiece in place. Repeat for the other side of the workpiece *(above)*.

4 Bending the arms

Once the horizontal bend has been made, quickly complete the two vertical bends. Keeping one hand on the bend, push one arm of the workpiece down and hook it behind the angle bracket, then clamp it and repeat for the other arm *(right)*. (The second arm will be more difficult to bend downward than the first; make the task easier by having a helper hold the first arm bent halfway while you bend the second arm, then go back and finish the bending on the first one.) Let the wood dry on the form overnight, then remove the workpiece and tie or clamp the ends together. Allow a week for the workpiece to dry completely.

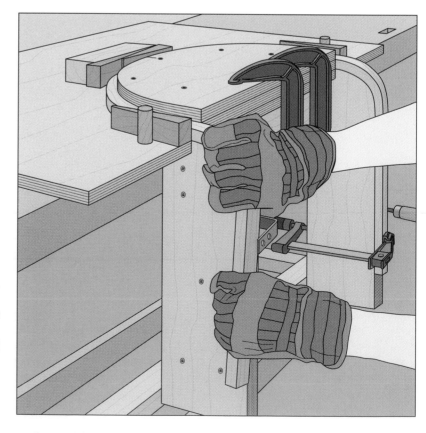

A WEDGE-MAKING JIG
FOR WOOD BENDING

The wedges used in two-plane bending *(page 51)* can be made quickly on the band saw with the jig shown at right. This particular setup will produce wedges with 8° angles. Refer to the illustration for suggested dimensions, making sure the hardwood runner fits snugly in the table miter slot.

Screw the runner to the underside of the base so the runner extends beyond the tabletop and the base sits squarely on the table when the runner is in the miter gauge slot; countersink the fasteners. Next, screw the fence to the top of the base; angle the fence at 4°. Set the jig on the table with the runner in the slot, turn on the saw, and cut through the base until the blade contacts the fence. Next, prepare the stop block by cutting a slot through the block for a machine bolt. Attach the block

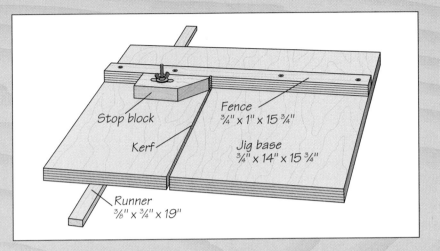

Stop block

Kerf

Fence
¾" x 1" x 15 ¾"

Jig base
¾" x 14" x 15 ¾"

Runner
⅜" x ¾" x 19"

to the base, adding a washer and wing nut. The block should be flush against the fence with the tip of its angled end aligned with the kerf.

For your wedge stock, cut a board as long as the desired length of the wedges. Position the jig on the saw table. Holding your stock with its edge flush against the fence and one end butted against the stop block, feed

the jig across the table. Make sure your hands are clear of the blade as you cut each wedge *(below)*. If you simply flip the workpiece between cuts on the band saw, all the wedges after the first will have 8° angles.

To produce thicker wedges, loosen the wing nut and slide the stop block slightly away from the kerf. Tighten the wing nut and cut the wedges.

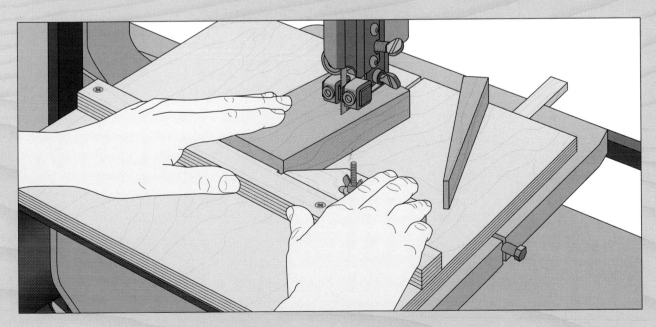

SHAKER BOXES

BENDING A SHAKER BOX

First produced in the 1790s, Shaker boxes were made in graduated sizes to hold household goods; when empty, they could be nested inside one another. The oval boxes remain popular today, and can be made easily from commercial kits. The box shown at left was made by craftsman John Wilson, of Charlotte, Michigan. He added a few luxurious refinements to the utilitarian yet elegant Shaker design, such as using bird's-eye maple for the box bands and a walnut burl veneer for the top.

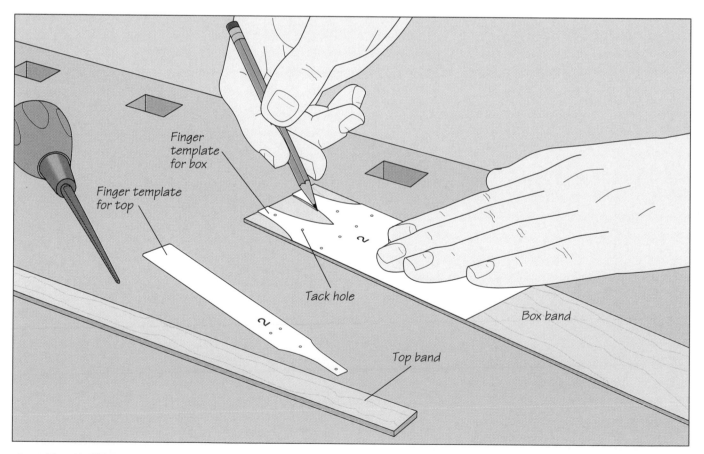

Finger template for box

Finger template for top

Tack hole

Box band

Top band

1 Cutting the fingers

To make a Shaker box from a commercial kit, first prepare the stock for the two bands—one for the box and one for the top. The bands are typically resawn from hardwood stock to a thickness of 1/16 inch. For best results, use straight-grained, quartersawn stock air-dried to a moisture content of 15 to 20 percent. Once the bands have been cut to size, use the proper-sized finger template to outline the fingers on the box band *(above)*, then mark the tack holes and drill them with a 1/16-inch bit.

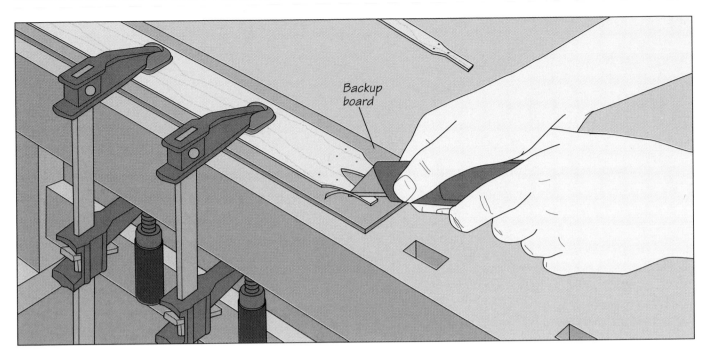

2 Beveling the fingers

Clamp the bands to a backup board and bevel the fingers with a utility knife. Holding the knife firmly with both hands, cut at an angle of 10° around the fingers *(above)*. Then taper the outside face of the opposite end of each band using a belt sander, starting the taper about 1½ inches in from the end. This will ensure a smooth overlap and uniform thickness once the bands are bent.

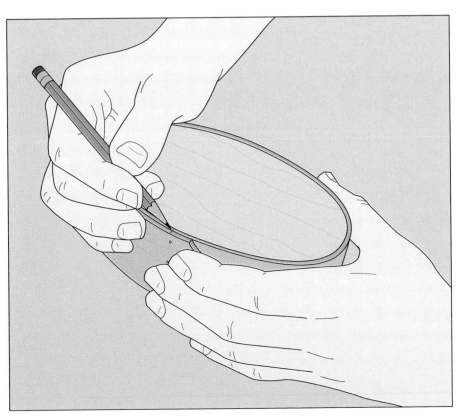

3 Marking the joint

Soak the box and lid bands in boiling water until they are soft—typically about 20 minutes. Remove the box band from the water and wrap it around the proper-sized box core so that the beveled fingers lap over the tapered end. Make a reference mark across the edges of the band where the ends overlap *(left)*. Keep the beveled fingers pressed tightly against the core to prevent them from splitting.

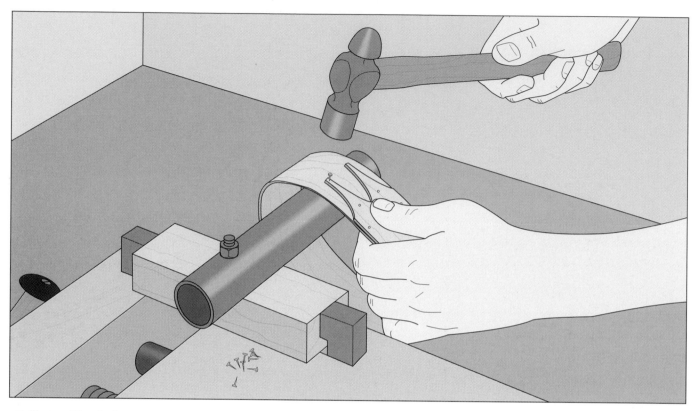

4 Tack-nailing the box

Working quickly, slip the band off the core, rebend it so that the pencil marks line up, and tack-nail it through the holes you drilled in step 1 using the appropriate copper tacks. To clinch the tacks inside the band, use a length of iron pipe clamped to your bench as an anvil *(above)*. Once the box bands are tack-nailed, place two shape-holders inside the band—one at each edge—to maintain the oval form as it dries.

5 Shaping the lid band

Using the process just described, shape and tack-nail the top band for the box lid, but use the drying box band as a bending form and shape-holder as it dries *(right)*. Allow two days for the two bands to dry. To complete the box, cut a lid and bottom from quartersawn stock to fit inside the bands, drill 1/16-inch pilot holes, and use toothpicks as pegs to secure the pieces.

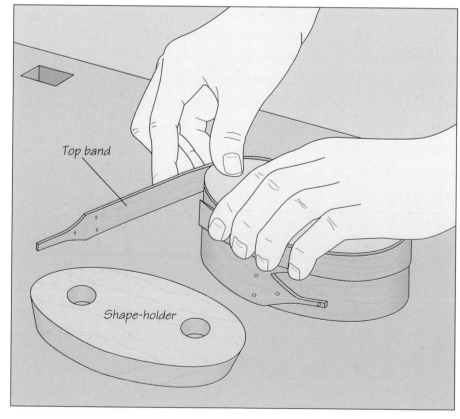

Top band

Shape-holder

LAMINATE BENDING

Wood does not have to be steamed to be bent; most hardwoods can be made pliable by cutting them into thin strips. In much the same way that veneer is laminated to a piece of core stock to create plywood, thin strips of resawn wood can be bent around a form and glued to create a new shape. The thinner the strip, the tighter the bend that can be made. There is one important difference between strip laminations and veneer lay up, however. Whereas veneer grain alternates with each layer for stability, the grain of all laminated strips is aligned in the same direction so that they move together and behave like a single piece of wood. When laminating wide panels, it is necessary to cross-band; otherwise, the panel will warp. Also, the grain of the outside faces must run in the same direction, for appearance and to keep the panel from twisting.

Like steam bending, lamination is an economical method of creating curved shapes; laminated workpieces can be made from a narrower board than it would take to band saw a similar curve, and can be made thinner because of the strength of the adhesive bonding parallel to the grain direction. Laminate bending also has a few advantages over steam: There is less setup time, any wood species can be used, and there is more control over the final shape. The biggest disadvantage is the glue lines that will appear if you wish to taper the piece. When choosing wood for laminating, select straight-grained, defect-free lumber. For a list of suitable woods, see the chart on page 43.

The Macassar ebony chair shown at right, produced by furniture maker Michael Fortune, features laminated curved arms and back legs.

MAKING A BENT LAMINATION

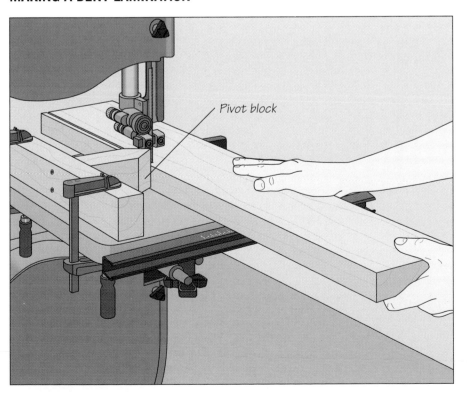

Pivot block

1 Resawing stock into strips
Cut the strips for a bent lamination from a hardwood board slightly longer and wider than the bent piece you wish to make. Set up a pivot block on the band saw as you would to cut veneer *(page 122)*. In this case, the pivot block is fastened to a shop-made rip fence. Position the fence for a width of cut slightly greater than ⅛ inch, as some stock will be removed by sanding (step 2). Press the stock flush against the tip of the pivot block as you feed the workpiece *(left)*. Near the end of the cut, move to the back of the table and pull the stock past the blade. After each pass, joint the cut edge of the workpiece to ensure that one side of every strip is perfectly flat and smooth. You can also use a table saw, cutting each strip to its final thickness and omitting the sanding procedure. **(Caution: Always use a push-stick and featherboards for this operation.)**

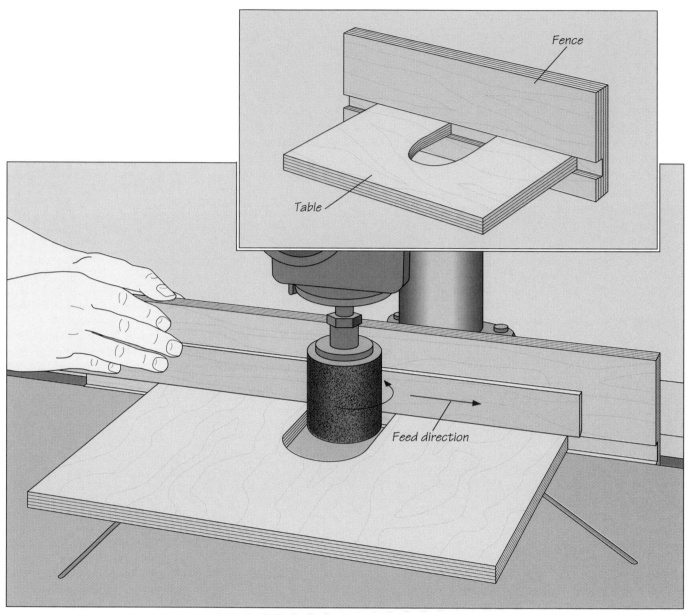

Fence

Table

Feed direction

2 Sanding the strips

The strips can be smoothed and reduced to their final thickness—typically ⅛ inch—on a radial arm saw equipped with the simple sanding jig shown in the inset above. To make the jig, cut the table and fence from ¾-inch plywood, sizing the pieces to fit your saw. Cut a slot out of one edge of the table large enough to accommodate the sanding drum you will use. Rout a ¾-inch-wide groove along the length of the fence, leaving ¾ inch of stock below the channel to slip into the saw table's fence slot. Insert the slotted edge of the table into the groove in the fence and screw the two pieces together. To sand the laminating strips, install a sanding drum with 50- or 60-grit paper in your saw, following the manufacturer's instructions. Slip the jig fence between the front and rear tables of the saw, positioning the opening in the base directly below the drum, then tighten the table clamps to secure the jig in place. Lower the drum so it is just below the top of the jig table and position the drum so the distance between it and the jig fence is slightly less than the thickness of the stock. Turn on the machine. With the jointed side of the strips butted against the fence, feed the stock slowly and continuously from left to right—against the sanding drum rotation—between the fence and drum (above). (Clamping featherboards to the jig table to press the stock against the fence can also help prevent gouging.) For each successive pass, reduce the gap between the fence and sanding drum by no more than ¹⁄₃₂ inch.

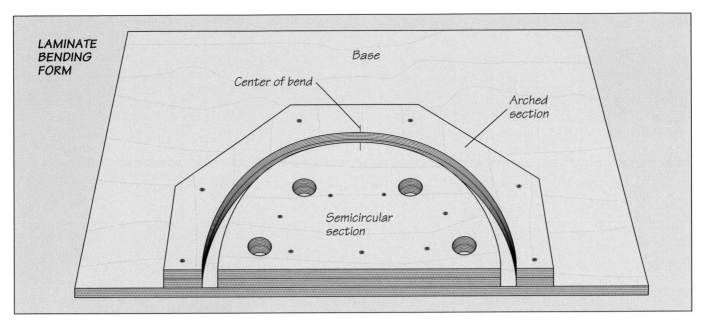

LAMINATE BENDING FORM

Base

Center of bend

Arched section

Semicircular section

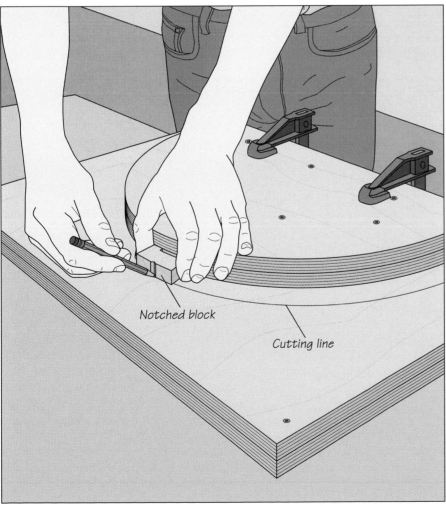

Notched block

Cutting line

3 Making a laminate bending form

To hold the laminates during glue up and apply even pressure along the bend, make a two-part form from two thicknesses of ¾-inch plywood screwed together and attached to a base *(above)*. Make the semicircular section as you would for steam bending *(page 47)*. To determine the required gap between the two parts of the form, dry-clamp the strips to be laminated together and measure their thickness. (Add an extra strip to your sum; this piece will serve as a backup strip.) Clamp the semicircular piece atop the second piece of plywood, aligning their edges, and cut a small wood block so that its width equals your measurement. Saw a small V-shaped notch in one edge of the block to accommodate a pencil, and a rectangular notch in the opposite side to provide two contact points that will ride around the curve. Then mark a cutting line for the arched section on the plywood piece *(left)* and cut along the line. Sand the cut edge of the arched section and apply a thin coat of wax to prevent the work from sticking to it. Cut the corners of the arched section and drill four holes in the semicircular part to accommodate clamps. Screw the semicircular piece to a base of ¾-inch plywood, and mark the center of the bend on its edge.

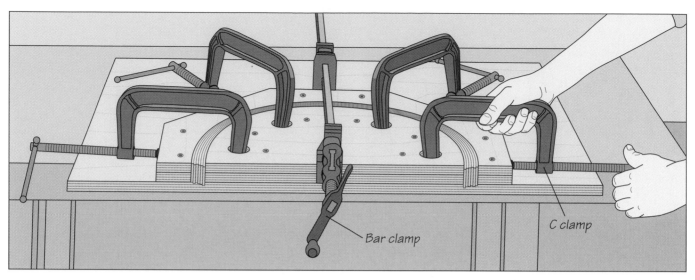

Bar clamp

C clamp

4 Gluing up the lamination

Stack the strips dry and mark a line across their center. Spread glue on one side of each strip and restack them, lining up the marks. Leave the backup strip dry on the outside to prevent the outer strip from splitting during glue up. Place the stack along the semicircular part of the form, lining up the center mark on the lamination with the one on the form. Set the form's arched section against the backup strip, pull it toward the semicircular section and install a bar clamp across the center of the bend. Secure the assembly with C clamps, working from the center to the ends *(above)*. Let the setup cure for 8 to 10 hours.

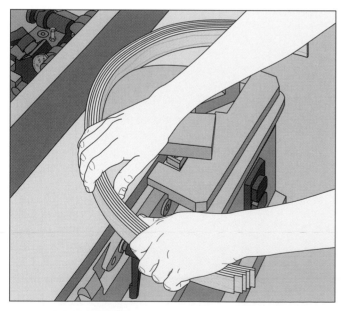

5 Jointing the lamination

Once the lamination is dry, remove it from the form and joint one edge. Slowly feed the workpiece across the cutters, applying pressure on the infeed side of the fence with your hands clear of the knives. Once the workpiece reaches the outfeed table, move your hands up and over to the outfeed side of the cutters, and apply pressure on the outfeed side *(above)*. Never position your hands directly over the cutters.

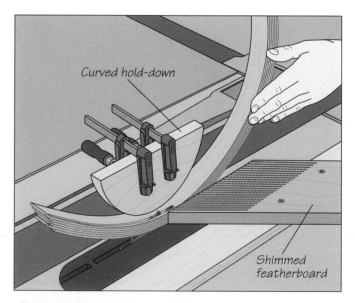

Curved hold-down

Shimmed featherboard

6 Ripping the lamination to width

Cut the lamination on your table saw with a shimmed featherboard secured to the table and a curved hold-down clamped to the rip fence. Set the featherboard slightly behind the blade so it will press the workpiece against the fence. Keeping your hands away from the blade, feed the stock convex face down until you are about halfway into the curve *(above)*; then move to the other side of the table and rotate the lamination while pulling it past the blade.

KERF BENDING

Kerf bending involves making a series of equally spaced saw cuts on one side of a workpiece, then bending and gluing the stock to produce a smooth curve along the opposite side. Kerf bending is commonly used where the kerfed side of a workpiece will remain hidden, and is popular for bending curves in larger sheet materials like plywood.

The spacing between the kerfs is determined by the desired radius of the curve. This figure must be precise, or the resulting curve will be uneven, but calculating the spacing is a simple process, as shown below.

Kerf bending reduces the strength of the workpiece because some of the wood is removed. If the workpiece has an exterior kerf bend, like the one in the photograph below, and will not be supported, fill the kerfs with a mixture of glue and sawdust to strengthen the piece.

Kerf bending can sometimes be used to esthetic advantage. The rounded mahogany picture frame shown at right turns the technique inside-out, exposing the kerfs that are usually hidden and integrating them into the design by inserting wedges of contrasting walnut.

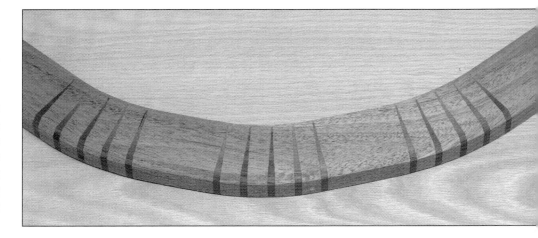

KERF BENDING A WORKPIECE

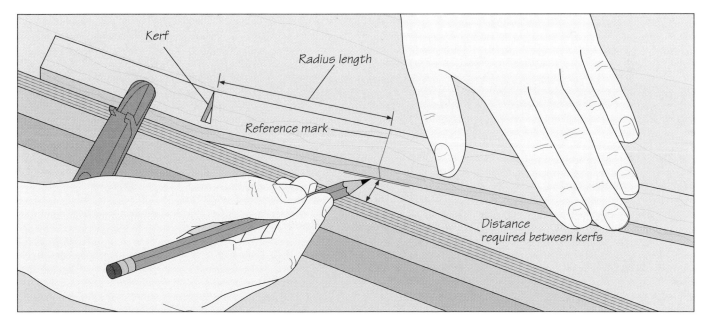

Kerf

Radius length

Reference mark

Distance
required between kerfs

1 Calculating the kerf spacing for an interior bend

Mark the radius of the desired curve on one face of a thin piece of waste wood the same width as the wood to be bent, starting about 3 inches from one end. At this end of the radius line, cut a kerf about three-quarters of the way across the waste piece; the kerf should be the same thickness as the kerf you will cut in the workpiece. With a try square, extend the second reference mark across the face of the waste strip and down one edge and clamp the strip flush with the perfectly straight edge of a scrap board. Then push the free end of the strip until the kerf closes, and make a mark on the scrap board where the reference line meets the board *(above)*. The distance between the edge of the board and the mark is the spacing required between kerfs.

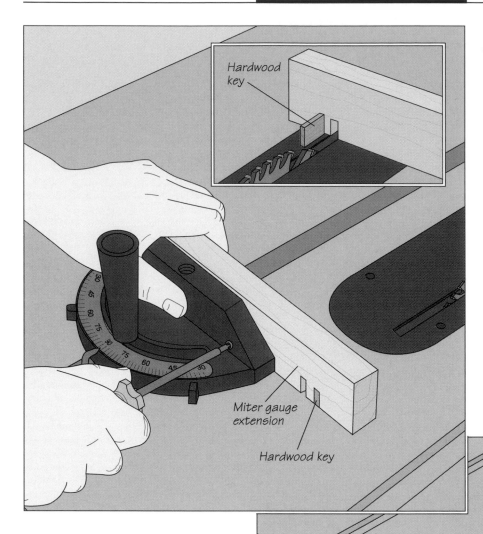

Hardwood key

Miter gauge extension

Hardwood key

2 Setting up the jig

To cut equally spaced kerfs in a workpiece, equip your table saw with this simple jig. Set the cutting height to ⅛ inch less than the workpiece thickness. Then screw a board to the miter gauge as an extension and feed it into the blade to kerf it. Unscrew the extension, shift it to the right by the distance you calculated in step 1, and refasten it to the miter gauge. Feed the extension into the blade to cut a second kerf. Remove the extension, and fit and glue a hardwood key into the first kerf so that the key projects about an inch from the extension (inset). Screw the extension back to the gauge so that the second kerf is in line with the blade (left).

3 Kerfing the workpiece

Butt one end of the workpiece against the key, holding an edge against the miter gauge extension. Feed the workpiece into the blade to cut the first kerf. To make the second cut, fit the kerf over the key, and continue cutting kerfs one after another (right) until you reach the opposite end of the workpiece.

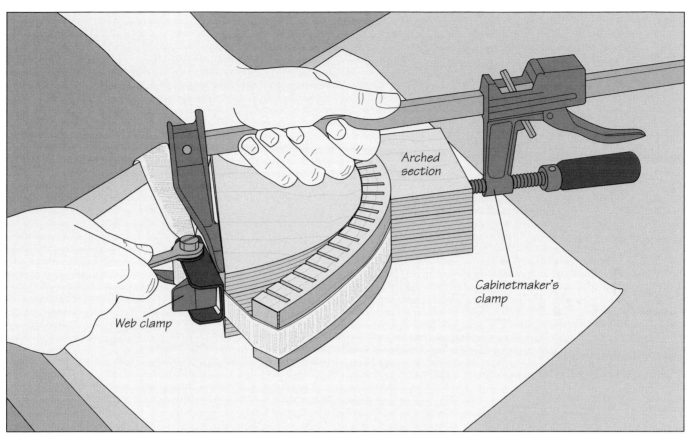

Arched section

Cabinetmaker's clamp

Web clamp

4 **Clamping the workpiece**
The kerfed workpiece can be bent around a two-part form cut to the desired radius using the technique on page 59. Work on a sheet of wax paper so the workpiece will not bond to your workbench. Apply glue in the kerfs, slip the web clamp between the unkerfed side of the stock and the arched section of the form, and tighten it until the stock begins to bend. Press the two parts of the form together with a cabinetmaker's clamp, and tighten it to apply pressure at the middle of the bend. Then tighten the web clamp *(above)* until the workpiece bends completely around the semicircular section.

SHOP TIP

Hiding kerfs in kerf-bent wood
If both sides of a kerf-bent workpiece will be visible, kerf bend two pieces and glue them together back to back as shown here. Glue the two pieces together using the two-part form shown in step 4 above. If desired, you can conceal the top and bottom with veneer or solid stock.

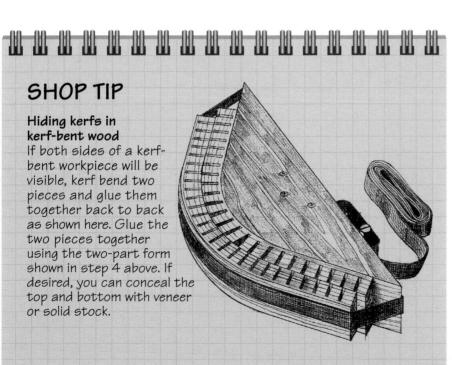

BENDING PLYWOOD

While kerfing remains as the most popular method of bending plywood panels to create items such as bowed door panels, curved cabinet sides, or round blanket chest lids, the task can also be done by bending ¼-inch or ⅛-inch plywood if the desired curve is shallow. The trick is to build the laminated component from two or more sheets of thin plywood sandwiched by the desired decorative face veneer. The only jig you require is a torsion box like the one shown below. The box distributes bending pressure equally over large laminated panels. The steps involved are similar to those used in making a laminate bending form *(page 59)*, and can be adapted to suit a variety of contoured shapes. For curves that are too severe for ¼-inch plywood, you can use bendable plywood or build your laminate from many layers of thin veneer.

Available at lumberyards under a variety of trade names and nicknames such as "Curve-Ply" and "wacky wood," bendable plywood is a three-ply sheet material typically between ⅛ and ⅜ inch thick. It features a flexible inner core sandwiched between two outer layers with parallel grain.

MAKING A BENT PLYWOOD LAMINATE

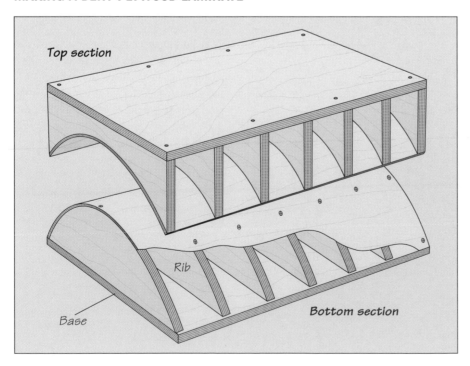

Top section

Bottom section

Rib

Base

1 Designing a torsion box
To make a curved plywood laminate, first build a torsion box. The jig shown at left is made from ¼- and ¾-inch plywood. It consists of two parts, reinforced by ribs, which fit together and apply uniform pressure on a panel. Both the top and bottom are screwed to base panels made from the thicker plywood; the curved panels of the jig are formed of thin plywood. The ribs must be contour-cut to the desired curve *(step 2)*, then the curved panels are fastened to the ribs *(step 3)*. The number of ribs needed depends on the size of the workpiece and the radius of the desired curve. As a general rule, the tighter the curve, the more pressure—and ribs— needed. The torsion box in the illustration, useful for bending moderate curves, features ribs at 3-inch intervals.

2 Cutting the ribs

A band saw can be used to prepare several ribs at a time; use the convex pieces for the bottom of the jig and the concave pieces for the top. Start by stacking several oversize blanks one atop the other and screw them together to keep their edges and ends aligned; make sure the screws will not be in the path of the blade when you saw the ribs. On the face of the top piece, draw two cutting lines: Make one equal to the desired radius to be bent; draw the second line parallel to the first, and separated from it by the thickness of the workpieces plus the two curved panels of the jig. Use Xs to indicate the waste area. To make the cuts, feed the blanks face up, sawing the concave ribs first *(right)*, then the convex ones.

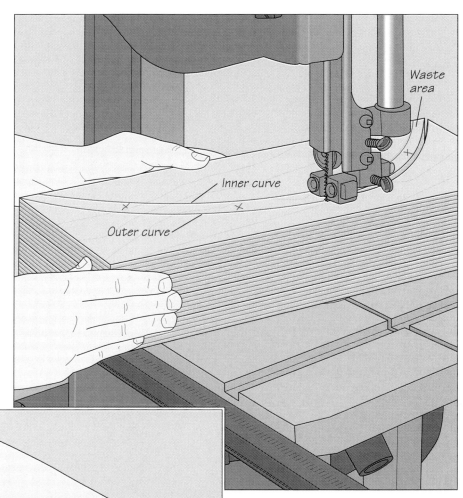

Waste area

Inner curve

Outer curve

3 Assembling the box

Once all the ribs are cut, screw them to their bases from underneath, spacing them about 3 to 4 inches apart. Then cut the two curved panels from ¼-inch or bendable plywood, and fasten them to the contoured edges of the ribs *(left)*, installing a screw every 3 inches. Countersink the fasteners and cover their heads with wood putty to ensure a smooth surface. Once both parts of the form are assembled, wax the top surfaces of the curved panels to keep the workpiece from sticking to the form.

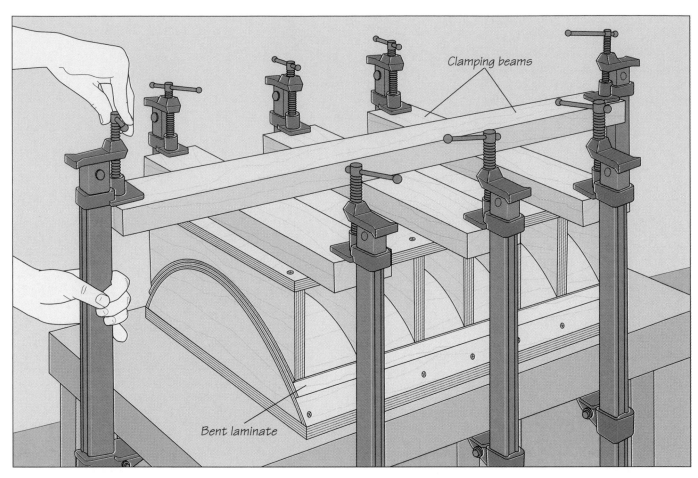

Clamping beams

Bent laminate

4 Gluing up the laminate

Glue up the curved laminate in the torsion box with bar clamps and a series of clamping beams cut from 2-by-4 stock. The beams serve to distribute the clamping pressure evenly. Apply glue to the mating surfaces, sandwiching the core sheets of plywood to be bent between the desired face veneers. Place the laminate between the two halves of the form. Set the clamping beams across the width of the box and clamp the assembly between them and the work surface. Working from the center out, tighten the clamps a little at a time until the lamination is bent snugly between the two forms. To apply pressure at the center of the bend, clamp another beam perpendicular to the others *(above)*. Let the setup cure for about 12 hours.

SHOP TIP

Veneering a serpentine surface
To veneer a contoured surface with more than one bend, such as the drawer front shown here, use sandbags or pillowcases filled with sand. For best results, start laying the bags on the middle of the surface, working your way out toward the ends. Since moderate heat accelerates the glue-curing process, keep the bags near a heater or shop stove as you prepare for the job.

COOPERING

Laminate bending with plywood can produce curved lids, doors, and panels. But if you want to shape the edge of your workpiece with a router, you will have to form the pieces out of solid stock. One way to do this involves a process known as coopering.

This technique was developed by barrel-makers, called coopers, who heated and softened beveled staves arranged in a circle around a fire and forced them into a cylindrical shape with metal hoops. Cabinetmakers have adapted the beveling idea and applied it to creating curved elements in their designs. Coopering is easy to do using a jointer with a tilting fence, as shown on the pages that follow.

Coopering creates a curved board by beveling wood strips at exactly the same angle on the jointer and then gluing them into a curved shape. Here, a woodworker uses a hand scraper to smooth the inside of a coopered blanket chest lid.

COOPERING A CURVED PANEL

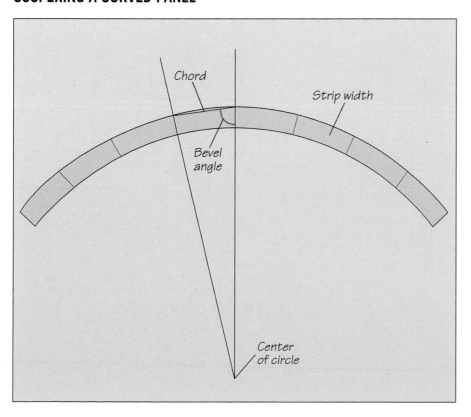

1 Calculating the strip bevel
To determine the bevel angle for the strips so they will form the proper curve when butted edge to edge, draw a full-scale sketch of the curved panel. Determine the width of the strips and mark their edges on your sketch; more strips will produce a smoother curve. Strips 2 inches wide work well for a chest lid, for example. Draw two lines connecting the edges of one strip to the center of the circle described by the curve. Then draw a chord across the outside of the strip *(left)*. The angle formed by the line drawn from the center of the circle and the chord is the angle at which you will need to bevel the strips.

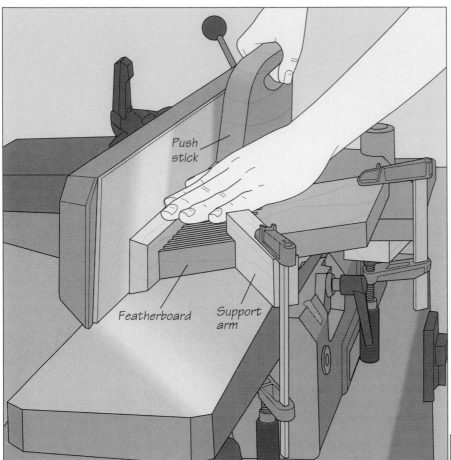

2 Beveling the boards on the jointer

Rip the stock, leaving the pieces ⅛ inch wider than necessary; this extra material will be removed by the jointer. (If you are working with stock cut from a single board, you may want to mark the ends of the boards in sequence so the original grain pattern will be preserved.) Set the jointer fence to the bevel angle you measured in step 1, tilting the fence toward the tables. Clamp a featherboard and support arm to the outfeed table. Bevel both edges of each strip, using a push stick to feed the work across the cutters *(left)*. Also cut several lengths of 1-by-2s for clamping pads to the same length as the strips.

3 Gluing the strips into pairs

Once all the strips have been beveled, edge-glue them in pairs, using bar clamps and the clamping pads to hold them as the adhesive dries. Install the clamps at 12- to 18-inch intervals, alternating between the top and bottom of the stock *(right)*. (If you are using strips cut from a single board, follow the numbers you marked on their ends to glue them up in the correct order.) If you have an odd number of strips, the remaining one can be glued up in step 4.

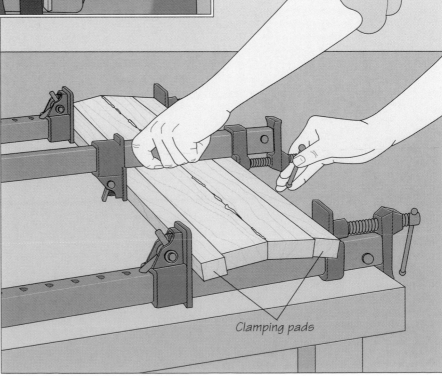

4 Gluing up half the curved panel

Once all the glued-up pairs of strips are dry, edge-glue one-half of the pairs together with bar clamps and clamping pads. To maintain downward pressure on the center of the bend and prevent it from popping out of the bar clamps, install a quick-action clamp at each end of the panel, securing it to the work surface. Repeat for the other half of the panel, including any remaining boards in the operation *(right)*.

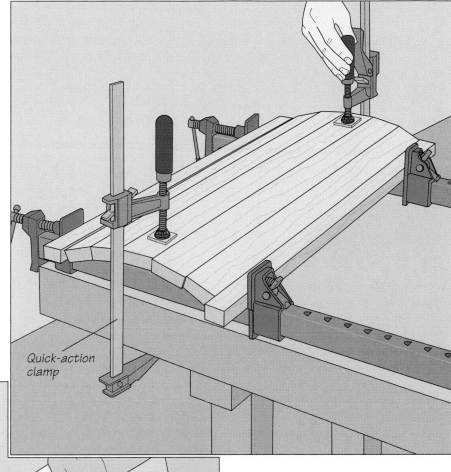

Quick-action clamp

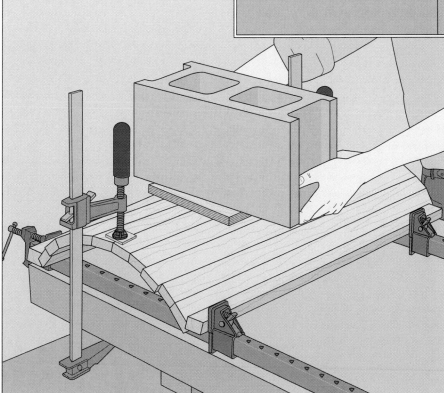

5 Final glue up

Glue up the two halves of the panel as you did in step 4; place a heavy weight, such as a concrete block, in the center of the panel to equalize the clamping pressure on the center joint *(left)*. Protect the panel with scrap wood. Once the glue has cured, use a handsaw to crosscut the panel to length.

CARVING

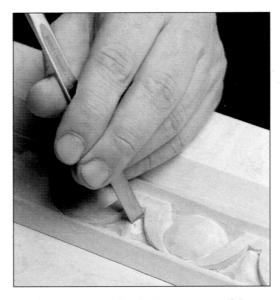

A gouge carves the sloping contours of the dart in a length of egg-and-dart molding. A narrow tool with a shallow sweep, or curvature, provides the most precise cut.

Of all the skills in woodworking, carving best represents a marriage between technical ability and artistic expression. For centuries, wood-carvers have wielded simple tools to transform wood blocks into objects they have seen in the world around them: leaves, shells, and folds of cloth, as well as figures. The wood-carving tradition has evolved, but the practice has remained remarkably little changed. In an age of power tools, the purity of a carver working on a simple block of wood equipped only with an array of hand tools holds an undeniable appeal.

Proper carving technique can be learned and honed with experience. Again, as with other woodworking techniques, the old admonition that "practice makes perfect" applies. But in practice carving builds more than dexterity. Good carving demands an ability to look at the world with a carver's eye, seeing the shapes and details of potential subjects in a block of wood. The carver needs to develop an accurate visual memory and an ability to notice subtle details of the object that is being reproduced. Master carver Ian Agrell discusses this in his essay on page 11.

The tools of the trade may at first overwhelm the novice: The selection available is immense. Commercial carving sets are seldom helpful, for they typically contain rarely needed tools and omit others that are essential. Fortunately for the beginner, few tools are needed to start carving. Even professional wood carvers, with hundreds of tools at their disposal, perform the bulk of their work with a dozen or so gouges, chisels, and knives. The basic tools are listed page 72.

As all professional carvers know, sharpening is the first essential step in practicing their craft. There are many sharpening techniques and tools, but all share the same goal —a razor-sharp cutting edge. A detailed discussion of how to sharpen and grind carving tools begins on page 77. Another requirement is finding suitable wood and securing it to a bench. Refer to the information starting on page 87.

The remaining pages of the chapter will carry you through some traditional and classical carving projects. Egg-and-dart molding *(page 91)* and fans and shells *(page 93)* can be applied to all types of furniture. Acanthus leaves *(page 98)*, linenfold panels *(page 101)*, and claw-and-ball feet *(page 106)* have been used to decorate furniture for centuries. Any of these projects is a suitable entry point into the venerable art of carving.

The linenfold panel shown at left, produced by a student at The School of Classical Woodcarving in Sausalito, California, is inspired by a design introduced to England in the late 15th Century. The panel suggests the symmetrical folds of draped altar cloths. The detailed lacework at the top of the piece is typical of the earliest examples of this style.

A COLLECTION OF CARVING TOOLS

Straight gouge
Features a curved cutting edge with a straight tip for carving relief and detail work

Skew chisel
Features a flat, angled cutting edge for fine detail work

Straight chisel
Flat-bladed carving tool with bevels on inside and outside surfaces for rounding convex surfaces and removing background

Fishtail gouge
The blade's flared tip is ideal for cleaning out corners and undercutting, particularly with limited clearance

Bent gouge
Similar to a straight gouge, but with a gradual curve along blade length; used primarily to clear waste from a concave surface

Dogleg chisel
Blade tip offset at 90° from blade shaft; used for paring flat recesses and working in restricted spaces

Tool roll
Made from leather or heavy-duty canvas with pockets for storing carving tools; handles are inserted into slots so that blades protrude

A CARVER'S BASIC TOOLBOX

Carving tools are available in a wide assortment of shapes and sizes. Fortunately, you can perform most tasks with a minimum number of tools. As a beginner, start stocking your inventory from the list of "work-horse" tools below. Specialty carving tools can be added to your collection as required. As shown on page 74, carving tools are classified according to the curvature and width of the blade.

No. 1 straight chisel: 5 mm, 16 mm, 25 mm
No. 3 straight gouge: 16 mm, 30 mm
No. 5 straight gouge: 5 mm, 12 mm, 20 mm, 25 mm, 35 mm
No. 7 straight gouge: 10 mm, 14 mm
No. 8 straight gouge: 7 mm, 13 mm, 25 mm, 35 mm
No. 9 straight gouge: 13 mm
No. 3 fishtail gouge: 12 mm
No. 11 veiner: 3 mm, 18 mm, 25 mm
No. 5 spoon gouge: 8 mm, 20 mm
No. 8 spoon gouge: 16 mm
No. 12 V-parting tool: 8 mm

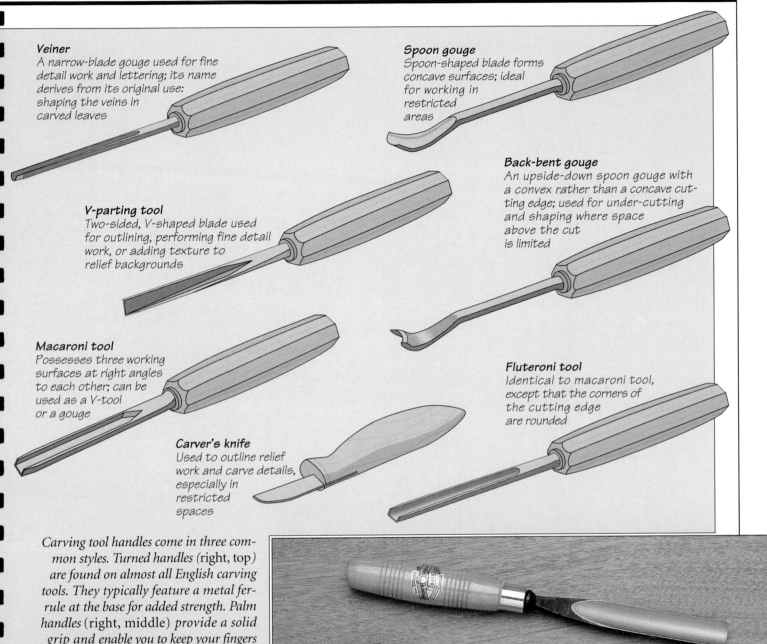

Veiner
A narrow-blade gouge used for fine detail work and lettering; its name derives from its original use: shaping the veins in carved leaves

Spoon gouge
Spoon-shaped blade forms concave surfaces; ideal for working in restricted areas

V-parting tool
Two-sided, V-shaped blade used for outlining, performing fine detail work, or adding texture to relief backgrounds

Back-bent gouge
An upside-down spoon gouge with a convex rather than a concave cutting edge; used for under-cutting and shaping where space above the cut is limited

Macaroni tool
Possesses three working surfaces at right angles to each other; can be used as a V-tool or a gouge

Fluteroni tool
Identical to macaroni tool, except that the corners of the cutting edge are rounded

Carver's knife
Used to outline relief work and carve details, especially in restricted spaces

Carving tool handles come in three common styles. Turned handles (right, top) *are found on almost all English carving tools. They typically feature a metal ferrule at the base for added strength. Palm handles* (right, middle) *provide a solid grip and enable you to keep your fingers close to the cutting edge for added control. Both handle types often have a flat surface on the underside that enables the tool to bite into the workpiece at a slightly lower angle and prevent the handle from rolling when it is set down on a work surface. Traditional Swiss- and German-designed octagonal handles* (right, bottom) *provide good control.*

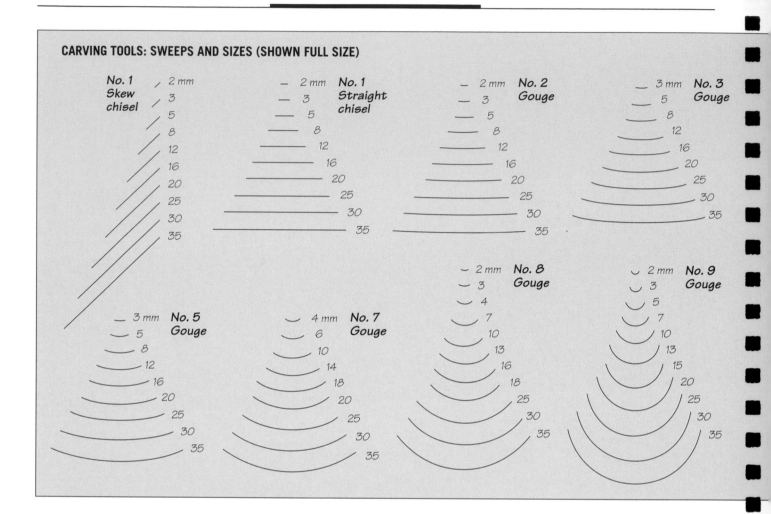

CARVING TOOLS: SWEEPS AND SIZES (SHOWN FULL SIZE)

No. 1 Skew chisel — 2 mm, 3, 5, 8, 12, 16, 20, 25, 30, 35

No. 1 Straight chisel — 2 mm, 3, 5, 8, 12, 16, 20, 25, 30, 35

No. 2 Gouge — 2 mm, 3, 5, 8, 12, 16, 20, 25, 30, 35

No. 3 Gouge — 3 mm, 5, 8, 12, 16, 20, 25, 30, 35

No. 5 Gouge — 3 mm, 5, 8, 12, 16, 20, 25, 30, 35

No. 7 Gouge — 4 mm, 6, 10, 14, 18, 20, 25, 30, 35

No. 8 Gouge — 2 mm, 3, 4, 7, 10, 13, 16, 18, 25, 30, 35

No. 9 Gouge — 2 mm, 3, 5, 7, 10, 13, 15, 20, 25, 30, 35

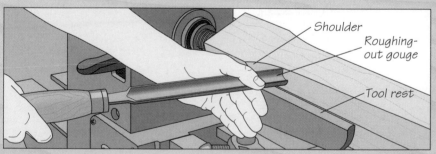

BUILD IT YOURSELF

A CARVER'S MALLET

A carving mallet can be easily made on a lathe. Start with a blank of face-glued stock larger than the finished dimensions of the mallet; hickory, maple, beech, and oak work well. Mount the blank on a lathe and set the tool rest as close as possible to the piece. Switch on the lathe and round the corners of the blank with a roughing-out gouge. Holding the tip of the gouge against the blank, slowly raise the handle until the cutting edge begins slicing into the wood and the beveled edge is rubbing against the stock. Rough-shape the mallet, moving the tool from side to side, leaving a shoulder where the head will join the handle (below). Finish shaping the blank using the same technique with a fingernail gouge (right). The handle of the

Shoulder
Roughing-out gouge
Tool rest

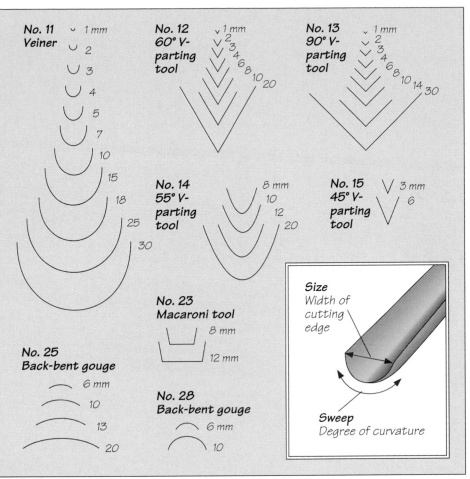

No. 11
Veiner
1 mm
2
3
4
5
7
10
15
18
25
30

No. 12
60° V-
parting
tool
1 mm
2
3
4
6
8
10
20

No. 13
90° V-
parting
tool
1 mm
2
3
4
6
8
10
14
30

No. 14
55° V-
parting
tool
8 mm
10
12
20

No. 15
45° V-
parting
tool
3 mm
6

No. 23
Macaroni tool
8 mm
12 mm

No. 25
Back-bent gouge
6 mm
10
13
20

No. 28
Back-bent gouge
6 mm
10

Size
Width of cutting edge

Sweep
Degree of curvature

Illustration courtesy of Woodcraft Supply Corp.

Carving tools are divided into three groups: Chisels, gouges, and V-parting tools. In each group, tools are distinguished by the shape of the blade (straight, spoon, V-parting, and so on); by the width of the cutting edge (2 mm to 35 mm); and by the degree of curvature, or sweep, of the blade (No. 1 to 28). The number increases with the degree of blade sweep. Straight, dogleg, and skew chisels all have flat blades and so are assigned No. 1. V-tools are assigned a number according to the angle, ranging from 45° to 90°. Straight, spoon, bent, and fishtail gouges share the same range of sweeps. Specialty tools like back-bent gouges and macaroni tools carry their own numbers.

mallet shown has a small nub at the end to provide a better grip.

Once the shaping is done, leave the mallet on the lathe, move the tool rest out of the way, and smooth its surface, starting with 80-grit sandpaper and moving to progressively finer grits. Then finish the mallet with tung oil; use small rags to avoid getting them snagged in the lathe. Finally, remove the mallet from the lathe, saw off the waste wood at the ends, and sand and finish the end grain.

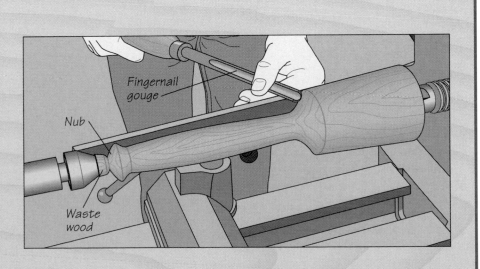

Fingernail gouge

Nub

Waste wood

CARVING ACCESSORIES

Carver's screw
Fastened through work surface to bottom of carving block

Bench hold-down
For clamping carving blocks on benchtop; fits in ¾-inch-diameter dog hole. Long arm allows easy access to all sides of workpiece

Router
Fitted with straight bit to remove background waste in relief carving

Bench dogs
Teamed with workbench vises to clamp stock; made of metal or wood. Tension spring keeps dog at desired height; after use, dog can be pushed below surface of benchtop

Hold-down clamp
Can be bolted to a work surface for securing carving blocks

C clamp
Secures blanks and backup boards to work surfaces. Available in sizes up to 18 inches; some have a deep throat for extended clamping reach

Trigger clamp
Secures carving blocks and backup boards; can be operated with one hand for quick adjustment. Padded jaws protect stock

The commercial vise shown at left serves well for carving. The vise rotates a full 360° and tilts up to 90°, providing access to all the surfaces of a workpiece. In addition, the front jaw tilts to secure tapered or oddly shaped stock. The vise comes with a built-in bench dog system for securing stock up to 13 inches wide.

Router plane
Also known as a granny's tooth; small hand plane, typically with a ¼-inch-wide blade for clearing waste from grooves and recesses, or for removing background waste in relief carving

TOOLS FOR SHARPENING

The number of stones and slips available for sharpening carving tools is almost as vast as the choice of tools themselves. Sharpening stones are generally divided into two groups according to the lubricant used: oilstones and waterstones. The lubrication serves to disperse ground particles and to prevent them from clogging the stone.

Naturally occurring oilstones, like Arkansas and Washita, have long been regarded as the finest sharpening stones in the world. Supplies of these stones are diminishing, however, and they are becoming prohibitively expensive. Man-made substitutes fashioned from aluminum oxide (India stones) or silicon carbide (Carborundum or Crystolon) are less expensive and virtually as effective, though they tend to wear out more quickly. An economical compromise is the use of an India stone for rough-sharpening and whetting, and an Arkansas slipstone for final honing.

Waterstones (also man-made) have become extremely popular with woodworkers. Although they cut much faster than oilstones, they do wear down more quickly and require a different sharpening technique. The following section on sharpening methods deals only with the use of oilstones.

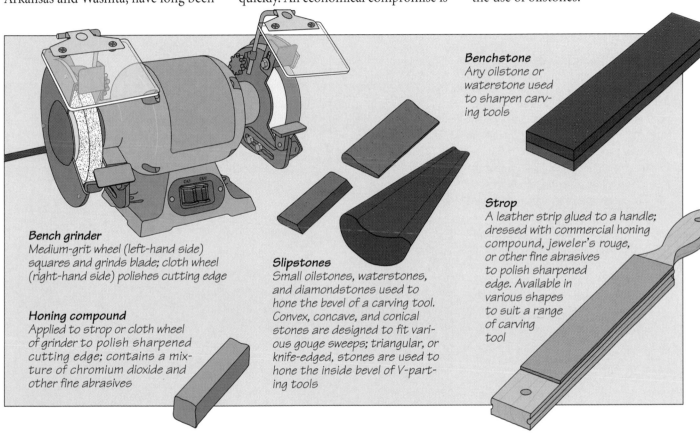

Benchstone
Any oilstone or waterstone used to sharpen carving tools

Bench grinder
Medium-grit wheel (left-hand side) squares and grinds blade; cloth wheel (right-hand side) polishes cutting edge

Honing compound
Applied to strop or cloth wheel of grinder to polish sharpened cutting edge; contains a mixture of chromium dioxide and other fine abrasives

Slipstones
Small oilstones, waterstones, and diamondstones used to hone the bevel of a carving tool. Convex, concave, and conical stones are designed to fit various gouge sweeps; triangular, or knife-edged, stones are used to hone the inside bevel of V-parting tools

Strop
A leather strip glued to a handle; dressed with commercial honing compound, jeweler's rouge, or other fine abrasives to polish sharpened edge. Available in various shapes to suit a range of carving tool

OILSTONES AND THEIR USES

OILSTONE	COLOR	TEXTURE	USES
Carborundum, Crystolon	Gray	100-200 grit	Grinding bevels; repairing damaged edges
Washita	Cream with darker streaks	350 grit	Whetting bevels; honing edges
India	Rust	90-600 grit	Whetting bevels; honing edges
Soft Arkansas	White with gray specks	800 grit	Honing edges
Hard Arkansas	White	1000 grit	Honing edges
Black Arkansas	Black	2000 grit	Honing or polishing edges

SHARPENING TECHNIQUES

Carving tools are supplied in various degrees of sharpness. In Great Britain, blades are given a basic grind before they are sold (*photo, page 79*), needing only to be honed and polished before use. North American manufacturers, on the other hand, supply carving tools in a wide range of conditions, from fully sharpened to crudely—and sometimes improperly—ground. The majority of new carving tools require some grinding before they can be whetted, honed, and polished to a razor-sharp edge. The two main goals of grinding are to thin the dull side of the cutting edge (*inset below*) and provide the correct bevel angle for the tool. To avoid drawing the temper as you grind the metal, a wet-wheel grinder is the best choice. If you are using a dry wheel, the tool must be cooled with water frequently.

Grind the bevel to an angle between 20° and 30° and make certain it is flat. The bevel must extend across the entire width of the blade and be square to the tool's edges. In general, a lower bevel angle will produce finer cuts, but its thin cutting edge will tend to break during use, particularly in harder woods. To strengthen the edge, hone an inside bevel with a slipstone (*page 85*). Carvers generally try to grind the lowest bevel angle that still resists breaking. Ultimately, only experimentation and experience will teach you what angle is best for your tools and style of carving.

GRINDING A CARVING TOOL

Grinding a gouge blade

Grind the bevel on a gouge blade using a grinder with a medium-grit wheel. Position the guard properly, adjust the tool rest to the desired bevel angle, and turn on the machine at its slowest setting. Holding the blade between the index finger and thumb of one hand, set the blade on the tool rest and advance it until the bevel is flat on the wheel. (If you wish to alter the bevel angle of the cutting edge, hold the blade against the wheel at the desired angle.) With your index finger against the tool rest, roll the blade on the wheel until the entire edge is ground (*right*). Continue, checking the blade regularly, until the cutting edge has been thinned (*below*) and the bevel angle is correct. Dip the blade in water occasionally to prevent it from overheating. Use the same technique for chisels and V-parting tools, but move the blade from side to side straight across the wheel.

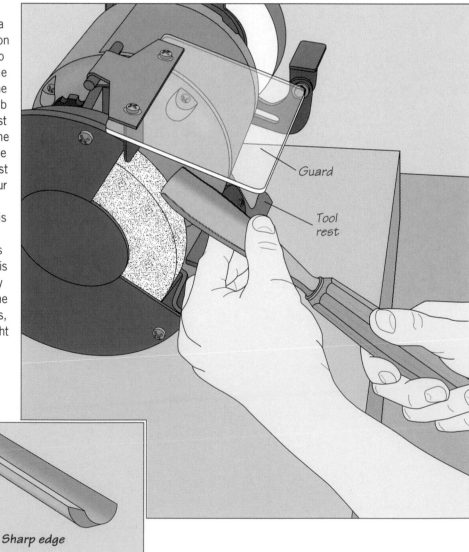

Guard

Tool rest

Dull edge   Sharp edge

Courtesy Veritas Tools 1990

Most carving tools require some grinding before they can be honed and polished to a razor-sharp edge. The British-made tools shown at right (from left to right, a chisel, a skew chisel, a gouge, and a V-tool) have been ground properly and are ready for final sharpening. The edges are fairly sharp with none of the dullness shown in the inset on the previous page. The bevels are flat and square to the edges of the tool.

BUILD IT YOURSELF

GOUGE-GRINDING JIG

The jig shown at right allows you to hold a gouge at the correct angle for grinding. The dimensions will accommodate most gouges. Cut the base and guide from ½-inch plywood. Screw the guide together and fasten it to the base with countersunk screws. Make the guide opening large enough for the arm to slide through freely.

Cut the arm from 1-by-2 stock and the tool support from ½-inch plywood. Screw the two parts of the tool support together, then fasten the bottom to the

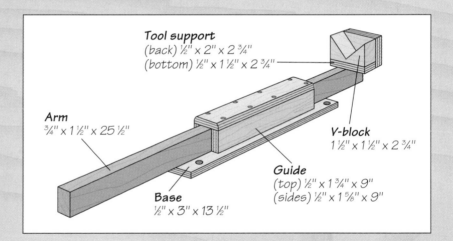

Tool support
(back) ½" x 2" x 2 ¾"
(bottom) ½" x 1 ½" x 2 ¾"

Arm
¾" x 1 ½" x 25 ½"

V-block
1 ½" x 1 ½" x 2 ¾"

Guide
(top) ½" x 1 ¾" x 9"
(sides) ½" x 1 ⅝" x 9"

Base
½" x 3" x 13 ½"

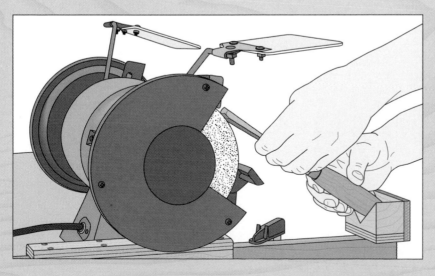

arm flush with one end. For the V-block, cut a small block to size and saw a 90° wedge out of one side. Glue the piece to the tool support.

To use the jig, secure it so the arm lines up directly under the grinding wheel. Seat the gouge handle in the V-block and slide the arm so the beveled edge of the gouge sits flat on the grinding wheel. Clamp the arm in place. Then, with the gouge clear of the wheel, switch on the grinder and reposition the tool in the jig. Roll the beveled edge across the wheel *(left)*.

S harp tools are essential for carving wood. Not only will they improve the quality of your work, they will also make it more enjoyable. Once you have ground the proper bevel on your tool *(page 78)*, you will need to hone and polish the blade before it is ready for work.

For carving chisels, both sides of the blade must be whetted, or honed, on a benchstone, and polished on a strop as shown at right and on page 81. The procedures for gouges and V-parting tools are a little more involved. In both cases, the outside bevel must be whetted. Depending on the quality of the bevel you produced on the blade, you may first have to use a medium stone and then move to a fine stone to achieve the desired sharpness. If the bevel has been properly ground, a fine stone should suffice.

The whetting process will raise a burr on the inside edge of the blade, which is honed away with a slipstone. This second process creates a slight inside bevel on the blade that strengthens the cutting edge. The angle of the inside bevel can be anywhere from 5° to 10°. Once the inside bevel is honed, the outside edge may need to be honed to a final edge with a slipstone. If the edge is sufficiently keen, however, both the inside and outside bevels are simply polished with a strop or the buffing wheel of a bench grinder. The steps for sharpening a V-parting tool are shown on page 82; for a gouge, see page 84.

SHARPENING A CARVING CHISEL

1 Honing the cutting edge
Lay a combination medium/fine stone on a plywood base, screw cleats alongside the stone to keep it from moving, and clamp the base to a work surface. Lubricate the stone with a few drops of light machine oil until it pools on the surface. Start by holding the blade with the outside bevel flat on the stone and slide the cutting edge back and forth until the rough grinding marks have disappeared *(above)* and a burr has formed on the inside edge. Flip the tool and repeat the procedure to hone the inside bevel. Both bevels should be about 20°.

SHOP TIP

A sharpening-stone holder
Carvers are constantly sharpening their tools. To make the process more convenient, build a permanent home for your stone. Outline the sharpening surface on a piece of solid wood large enough to be clamped to your bench. Then plow a recess within the outline using a router fitted with a straight bit; make the depth of the recess slightly more than one-half the thickness of the stone. Square the corners of the recess with a chisel and store the stone in the holder. When you need to do some sharpening, simply secure the board to your workbench.

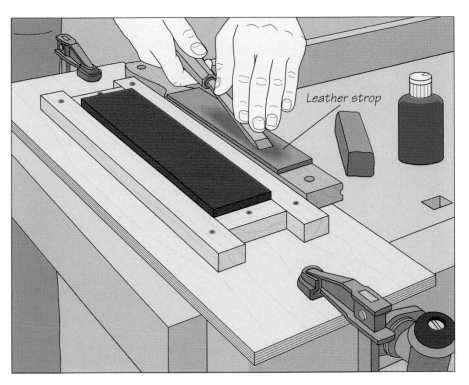

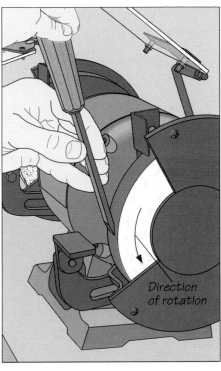

Direction
of rotation

Leather strop

2 Polishing the cutting edge

Use a leather strop or the buffing wheel of a bench grinder to polish both sides of the blade. If you are using a strop, you can fasten it to the base alongside the sharpening stone. Apply a light coating of polishing compound to the strop, hold the chisel with the outside edge on the leather, and draw the chisel toward you in long strokes, keeping the bevel flat *(above, left)*. Lift the tool at the end of each stroke. To polish a blade with the buffing wheel, hold the chisel almost vertically, with the bevel flat against the buffing wheel *(above, right)*. Move the chisel from side to side slowly as the wheel polishes the bevel. Whether you are using the strop or the wheel, continue until the burr remaining from the honing process disappears and the bevel is polished to a fine edge. Repeat on the other side of the blade.

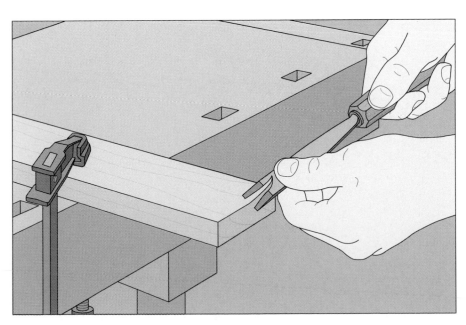

3 Testing for sharpness

There is no guarantee that the first sharpening of the blade will produce the keen edge required for carving. When you have completed steps 1 and 2, clamp a piece of pine or another softwood to the work surface and cut across the grain of the board. The blade should shear the wood cleanly without tearing out the fibers. Also note the sound that the blade produces; a razor-sharp carving tool will make a clean, hissing sound as it slices through the wood.

SHARPENING A V-TOOL

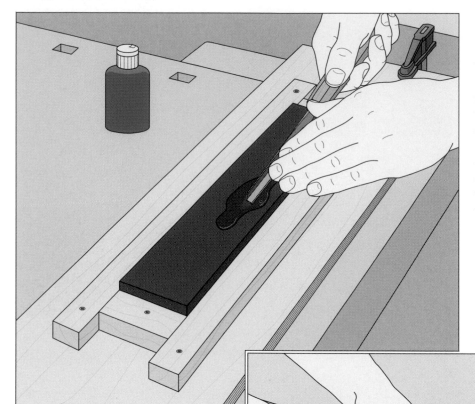

1 Whetting the outside edges
Sharpen each side of a V-tool separately. Hone one outside bevel as you would a chisel *(page 80)*, moving the blade back and forth along the length of a saturated oilstone and keeping the bevel flat on the stone. Repeat on the other side of the V *(left)*. Stop working when you have removed the rough marks from the ground edge and a small burr forms on the inside of the edge. To feel for the burr, run your finger gently across the inside edge of the blade.

2 Removing the hook
When you sharpen the outside bevels of a V-tool, a hook of excess metal will form at the apex of the V *(inset)*. This hook must be ground away before you hone the inside bevel in step 3. Holding the tool on the stone, roll the corner across the surface *(right)*. Move the tool from end to end along the stone until you wear away the hook and an outside bevel forms at the apex of the V. As much as possible, try to blend the bevel with the outside bevels on the sides of the V, forming one continuous beveled edge. This process will create a burr in the center of the inside edge, which is removed in step 3.

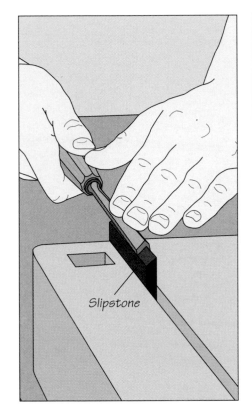

Slipstone

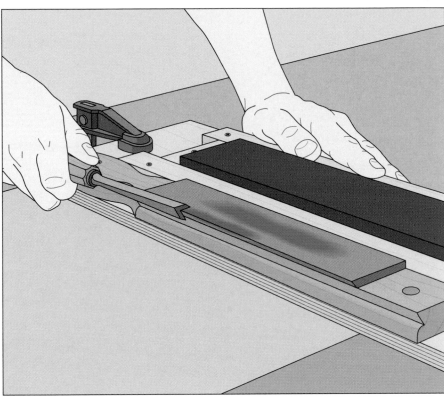

3 Honing the inside bevel
To remove the burr formed in steps 1 and 2, and hone an inside bevel, use a triangular slipstone that matches the angle of the V-tool blade as closely as possible. Clamp the stone securely in a bench vise and saturate it with oil. To avoid crushing the stone, do not over-tighten the vise. Then, with only the end of the blade's inside edge in contact with the stone, draw the tool forward and back applying light downward pressure (above, left). Check the inside edge of the blade periodically until the burr is removed and a slight inside bevel forms. To finish, polish the outside of the edge with a leather strop or a bench grinder polishing wheel (page 81). To polish the inside edge, cut the side of a commercial strop to match the interior angle of the V-tool and draw the tool along the angled edge (above, right).

SHOP TIP

Slipstones and strops for inside edges
The inside edges of carving tools—particularly gouges and V-tools—can be difficult to hone and strop, if you do not have a slipstone or strop of the correct shape. You can fashion a substitute for honing a gouge by wrapping a dowel with 600-grit sandpaper (near right). For V tools, attach the paper to a piece of scrap wood with an outside edge shaped like the inside angle of the blade. Use glue to secure the sandpaper in place. Contoured strops can be improvised by fastening a strip of leather to a suitably shaped wood block. A simpler option is to fold a strip of leather to fit the inside edge of the gouge or V-tool (far right).

SHARPENING A GOUGE

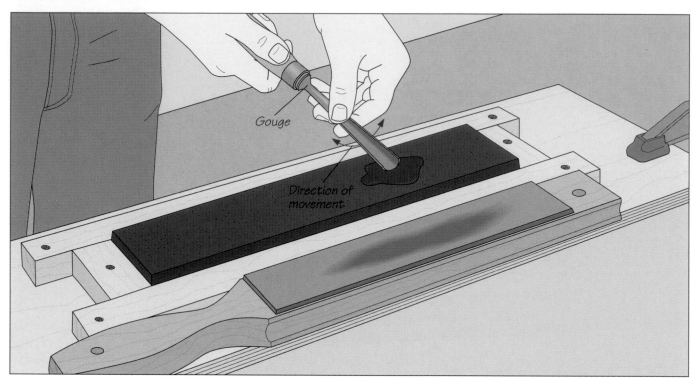

Gouge

Direction of movement

1 Whetting the outside bevel
Saturate an oilstone as you would to sharpen a chisel *(page 80)*, then set the outside bevel of the gouge flat on the stone. Starting at one end, move the blade back and forth along the stone with a rhythmic motion, simultaneously rolling the tool so the entire bevel contacts the sharpening surface *(above)*. Avoid rocking the blade too far, as this will tend to round over its corners and blunt the cutting edge. Continue until the bevel is smooth and a burr forms on the inside edge of the blade. The same technique is used to sharpen a front-bent, or spoon gouge, but you will need to hold the tool at a much higher angle to keep the bevel flat on the stone *(right)*.

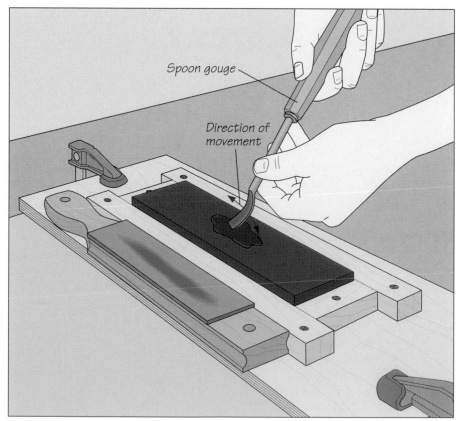

Spoon gouge

Direction of movement

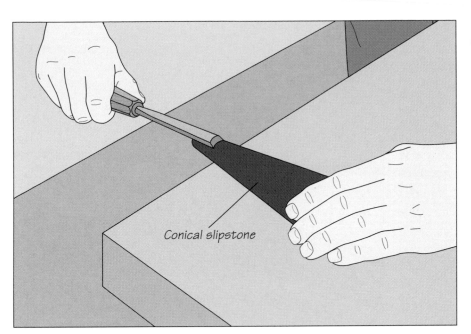

Conical slipstone

2 Honing an inside bevel
Once you have sharpened the gouge blade's outside bevel, use a conical slipstone to hone a slight inside bevel on the blade and remove the burr formed in step 1. Put a few drops of oil on the cutting edge of the gouge, then move the blade away from you across the stone. To avoid dulling the outside edges of the blade—and bringing the cutting edge close to your fingers—the blade should only contact the narrow portion of the stone *(left)*. Continue until the burr is removed and an inside bevel of 5° to 10° forms.

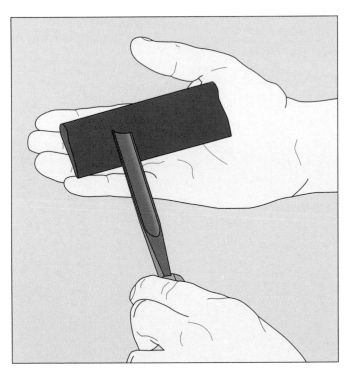

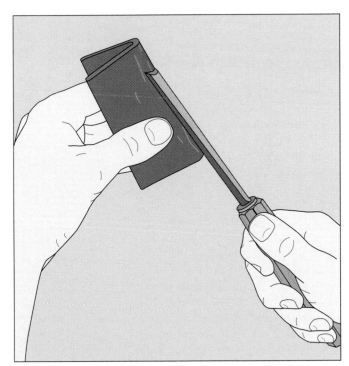

3 Refining the outside bevel
Use a fine slipstone to refine the gouge's outside bevel and remove any burr that may have formed during sharpening. Apply a few drops of oil to the cutting edge, then hold the slipstone in one hand and set the bevel flat on its surface. Draw the tool from side to side along the stone, rotating the blade to hone the bevel *(above)*. To protect your hand, work only in the middle portion of the stone. Continue honing until the burr is worn away.

4 Polishing the inside bevel
Use a folded piece of leather to strop the inside bevel of the gouge. Spread some polishing compound on the leather and fold it so its edge matches the inside curve of the gouge. Draw the blade along the leather repeatedly to polish the inside bevel *(above)*. You can also do the polishing using a shaped wood scrap *(page 86)*.

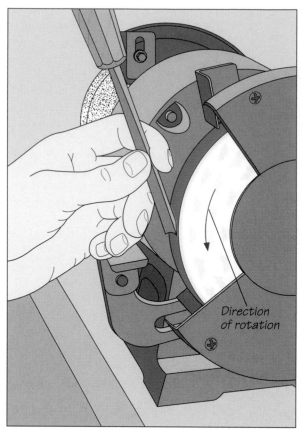

Direction of rotation

5 Polishing the outside bevel

Use a felt wheel on a grinder or a leather strop to polish the outside bevel of the gouge. To use a wheel, move the tool rest out of the way, turn on the tool, and hold a stick of polishing compound against it for a few seconds. Then, holding the gouge handle firmly in your right hand, pinch the blade with the fingers of your left hand and set the bevel flat against the wheel. Making sure the blade only contacts the lower half of the wheel, lightly roll the tool across the wheel to polish the bevel *(above, left)*. If you use a strop, spread some polishing compound on it, then use the same rolling technique shown in step 1 to polish the outside bevel *(above, right)*. Check the inside bevel; if a burr has formed, repeat step 4.

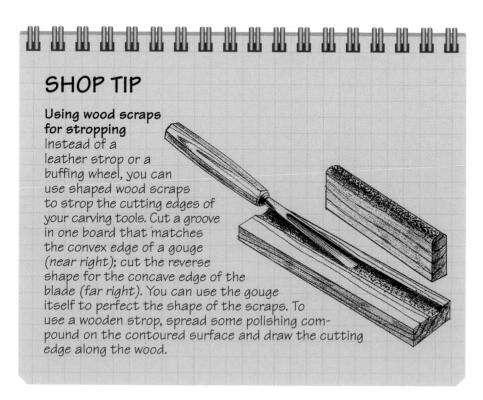

SHOP TIP

Using wood scraps for stropping
Instead of a leather strop or a buffing wheel, you can use shaped wood scraps to strop the cutting edges of your carving tools. Cut a groove in one board that matches the convex edge of a gouge *(near right)*; cut the reverse shape for the concave edge of the blade *(far right)*. You can use the gouge itself to perfect the shape of the scraps. To use a wooden strop, spread some polishing compound on the contoured surface and draw the cutting edge along the wood.

Once your tools are sharp, carving requires little preparation other than selecting a suitable wood for your project. The chart below lists a number of carving woods and their relevant characteristics. In general, soft, fine-textured woods with straight grain are best for small projects and detailed work. Dense hardwoods with fine textures accept details well, but require greater force to cut.

Once you have chosen your wood, use carbon paper or a graphite tracing to transfer your pattern to the carving block (*page 88*). Keep the pattern on hand after you have drawn it on the workpiece so that you can continue to transfer details to the wood as the carving progresses.

Securing your work is the final step before carving. Several effective methods are shown starting on page 88.

Finally, remember that a well-honed carving tool can inflict a serious wound. As much as possible, keep your hands behind the cutting edge and cut away from your body. And, for the sake of your safety and your work, do not use tools with dull or nicked blades.

The contours of a cabriole leg are shaped with a spokeshave. The leg is held in a bar clamp, which is secured to the work surface by a handscrew and two quick-action clamps. This setup exposes the entire front surface of the leg for shaping.

CARVING WOODS

WOODS	CHARACTERISTICS
Apple	Reddish brown to light red; hard with fine grain; carves well
Basswood	Creamy white darkening to creamy brown; soft with fine texture; carves very well
Birch	Creamy white to pale brown; hard with fine texture; straight-grained pieces carve well
Butternut	Medium light brown; moderately soft with somewhat coarse texture; carves very well
Cedar, aromatic	Reddish brown; moderately soft, very fine-textured; carves well
Cherry, black	Reddish brown to deep red; hard with fine texture; carves moderately well
Holly	White to grayish white; very fine texture; carves well
Jelatong	Light yellowish white; soft, very fine-textured; carves exceptionally well
Mahogany, Honduras	Light reddish brown to medium red; hard with medium coarse texture; carves well
Maple, soft	Cream to light brown; moderately hard with fine texture; carves well
Oak, white	Light tan with yellowish tint; hard with coarse texture; carves with difficulty
Padauk	Deep red to purple-brown with red streaks; hard with moderately coarse texture; carves moderately well
Pear	Pinkish brown; hard with very fine texture; carves very well
Pine, sugar	Light cream; soft with fine texture; carves very well
Poplar	White sapwood to pale brown heartwood; soft with fine texture; carves well
Purpleheart	Deep purple; hard with moderate to coarse texture; carves moderately well
Rosewood, Indonesian	Golden brown to dark purple-brown with black streaks; hard with medium texture; carves moderately well
Sycamore	Pale reddish brown; hard with fine grain; carves moderately well
Teak	Golden brown to rich brown with darker streaks; hard with coarse texture; carves well
Walnut	Dark brown to purplish black; moderately hard with medium coarse texture; carves very well

TRANSFERRING A PATTERN TO A WORKPIECE

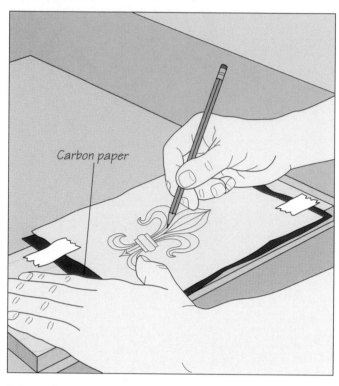

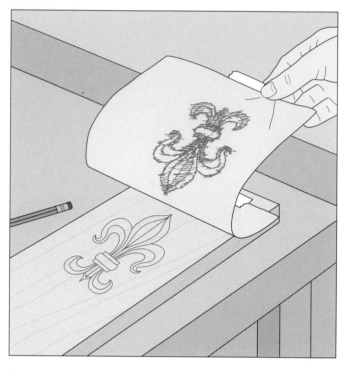

Using carbon paper

Copy the design to be carved on a piece of paper, then lay a piece of carbon paper carbon-side-down on the workpiece over the desired location of the carving. Lay the design on the carbon paper, tape the sheets to the workpiece, and use a sharp pencil to trace the outline *(above)*. The carbon paper will transfer the outline to the carving block.

Using a graphite tracing

As an alternative to carbon paper, transfer your pattern using a graphite tracing. Draw the design on a piece of paper. Then, using a fairly soft pencil (No. 2 or softer), blacken the back of the sheet. Tape the paper design-side-up to the workpiece and use a sharp pencil to trace the design. Stop partway through and lift off the paper to check that the design is being transferred to the workpiece.

SECURING THE WORKPIECE

Using a carver's screw

Specially designed to clamp a carving block to a work table, the carver's screw shown at right is fastened to the block and to the table. Start by boring a pilot hole for the screw in the bottom of the workpiece; bore a clearance hole through the table near one edge. Attach the screw to the block, slip the screw through the hole in the table, and turn the tightening knob until the block is secure on the work surface. Loosen the tightening knob to rotate the workpiece. When the carving is completed, plug the hole in the workpiece.

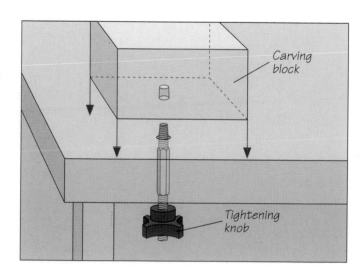

Using clamps
To secure a flat carving block to a work surface, glue it to a wood base, then secure the assembly with C clamps *(above)*. The base should be wider and longer than the workpiece. Place newspaper between the base and the carving block; this will enable you to pull the pieces apart easily when the carving is completed. Let the glue cure for at least an hour before carving.

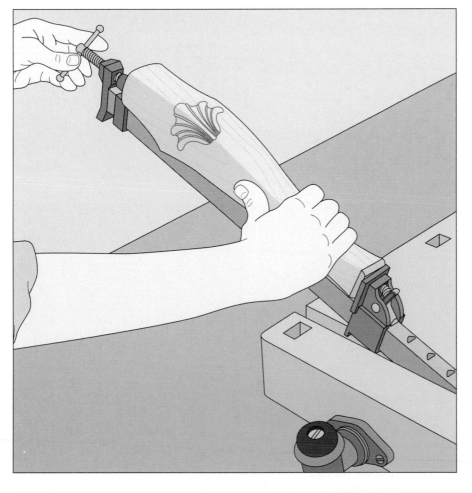

Securing irregularly shaped work
To clamp down awkwardly shaped workpieces like the cabriole leg shown at left, begin by securing the leg in a bar clamp. Then fix the clamp in a vise. Rotate the leg in the clamp as necessary.

BUILD IT YOURSELF

Wedge
1" x 1" x 3 ¼ "

Base
½" x 13" x 18 ½"

Edging strip
1" x 1 ½" x 18 ½

Carving
block

Spacer
1" x 2 ¼" x 15"

Clamping cleat
1" x 1 ½" x 18 ½"

A JIG FOR SECURING THIN WORK
The benchtop jig shown at left allows you to clamp a thin carving blank. Cut the base from ½-inch plywood and the remaining pieces from solid stock. Refer to the illustration for suggested dimensions, but be sure the base is longer than the workpiece and the spacer is long enough to butt against its entire front edge. The edging strips should be thicker than your stock. Screw them along the edges of the base and fasten two wedges flush against one strip as shown. Screw a cleat along the bottom of the base so the jig can be clamped in a vise. Set your stock on the base, butting one edge against the edging strip opposite the wedges. Butt the spacer against the opposite edge and slide the two loose wedges between the spacer and the fixed wedges. Tap the wedges tight to apply clamping pressure *(left)*.

To improve their efficiency, wood-carvers traditionally start a project by laying out all the tools they plan to use along the far edge of the carving block. The tools are positioned by frequency of use, with the most-often used on the left, and the less frequently used tools on the right. The blades face the carver for quick recognition. At each step of the carving process, the tools that are immediately involved are positioned alongside the left-hand end of the workpiece with their blades facing away.

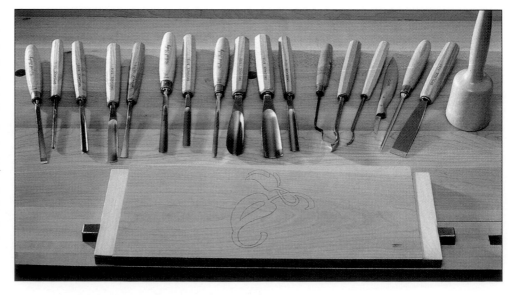

CARVED MOLDINGS

Carved moldings have been used to decorate furniture for centuries. In fact, experts are able to determine when and how a molding was cut by looking at its style and shape. The most common carved molding styles include the Gothic, which is deep-cut with a wide range of irregular shapes, and the Renaissance and Jacobean varieties, which feature more uniformly patterned work, built up from a fixed sequence of shallow cuts.

The first requirement for carved molding is a molding blank formed from an appropriate-size piece of stock. You can make a blank by hand with gouges, but for long sections, it is quicker to use a router or shaper. Before carving the molding, begin on a test piece and establish the sequence of cuts that will provide the desired result. For example, to produce the egg-and-dart molding shown on this and the follow-ing page, outline the eggs first *(steps 1 and 2)*, then shape them *(step 3)*, and finally carve the darts *(step 4)*. As a rule of thumb, molding should be carved with as few cuts as possible, making each one clean and decisive. Try to design the molding to suit the sweeps, or curves, of your tools, rather than the other way around. Carve one set of elements, such as the eggs, along the entire length of molding before changing tools and carv-ing the second series of elements. This will streamline the carving process and help give the result uniform appearance.

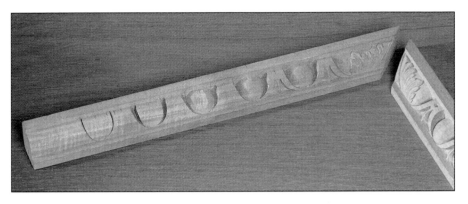

The egg-and-dart pattern shown above was carved in ovolo-shaped molding. The piece on the right is finished; the sample piece on the left shows the progression of required steps. Acanthus motifs at the corner will allow the mitered ends to butt together cleanly.

CARVING AN EGG-AND-DART MOLDING

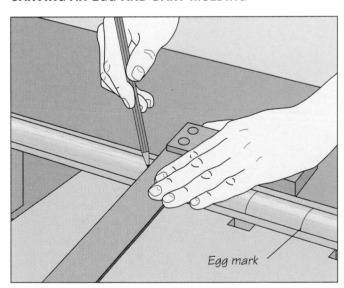

Egg mark

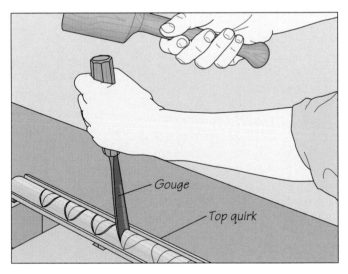

Gouge

Top quirk

1 Marking the eggs
Prepare a carving blank; the one shown above has an ovolo design—a type of quarter-round bordered by ridges called quirks. Secure the blank to your workbench, using bench dogs to keep the entire top face accessible. Mark the center of the eggs along the length of molding using a try square and a pencil *(above)*. Space the marks at intervals of about 2½ inches.

2 Outlining the eggs
Once you have marked the location of the eggs, use a gouge to outline their edges. Choose a gouge with a sweep that matches the desired curvature of the eggs. Holding the tool with the corner of the cutting edge just touching the top quirk, tap the handle lightly with a mallet to cut the outline around the egg. The cuts should slope slightly inward toward the center. Repeat the cuts to outline the remaining eggs along the length of molding *(above)*.

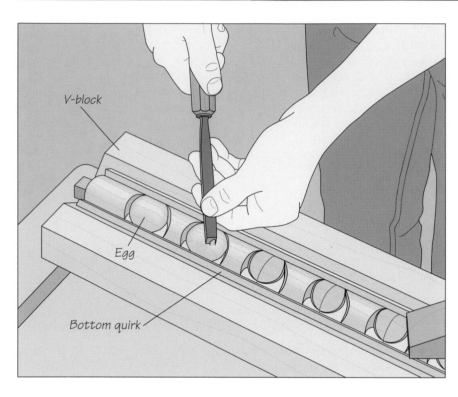

V-block

Egg

Bottom quirk

3 Shaping the eggs

Cut a 90° V-block jig on the table saw to hold the blank securely while allowing access to its top face. Clamp the molding in the V-block and use bench dogs to hold the block on the bench. With the same gouge used in step 1, make a vertical cut to widen the outline around the eggs. The width of the cut should be ¼ inch at the bottom quirk, gradually narrowing until it closes up at the top quirk. Once all the eggs are outlined, they can be shaped with a shallow-sweep (No. 3 or 4) straight gouge. Starting with the gouge nearly horizontal, raise the handle slowly as you carve from the top down to round the sides of each egg to the outline. Use only hand pressure except where difficult grain demands light taps with a mallet. Carve each egg the same way, then use a narrow gouge or carving chisel to give the eggs a final shaping *(left)*.

4 Carving the darts

Each dart consists of a central ridge flanked on either side by a triangular hollow. The hollows are carved with three cuts, producing a curved triangular chip which should come away easily. First, outline the darts between the eggs with a pencil. Then, using a gouge with the appropriate sweep, carve the curved outside edges of all the hollows. Holding the tool vertically, tap it with a mallet to cut to the desired depth, then repeat the cut on the other side of the dart *(right)*. Once all these curved cuts are made, use a straight chisel to carve the sides of the central ridges. Angle the tool at about 60° to start and lower the handle slightly as you tap the blade with a mallet. This will create a curved slope on each side of the ridges. Continue the cut until the blade meets the curved edge of the hollow. Make the last cuts with a small carving knife along the bottom edge of the hollows—flush with the top quirk—on each side of the dart *(inset)*. Wedge the waste chip out of the hollow with the knife.

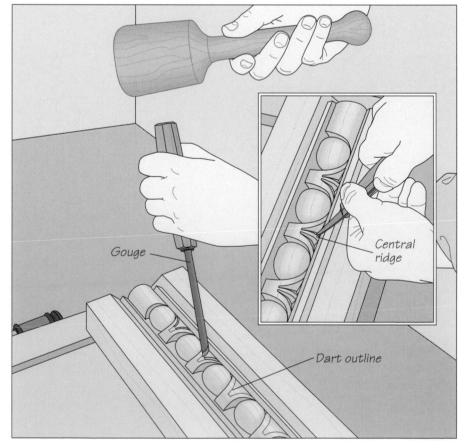

Gouge

Central ridge

Dart outline

FANS AND SHELLS

Scallop shells, sunbursts, and fans used in furniture making reached a pinnacle of popularity in the 18th Century. Then, as now, they were used extensively to adorn Queen Anne, Georgian, and Chippendale furniture, particularly on the fronts of central drawers and the knees of cabriole legs.

Simple fans, like the Queen Anne fan illustrated below, are relatively easy to carve and they lend themselves to a wide assortment of applications. For this reason, a fan is an ideal starting point for the beginning carver. However, care is needed, for the layout and planning of the cuts is particularly important, and it is crucial that the carving be suitably sized for the piece of furniture. The steps for carving a fan begin on page 94.

Fans and shells can either be carved directly on the furniture or shaped on a separate piece of wood, cut off, and glued

in place–also known as applied sculpture. Once you know where the cuts will be, the actual carving is relatively straightforward. As with molding, make one set of cuts across the entire workpiece before changing tools to make the next series of cuts. This will bring the entire piece to completion progressively, rather than one small section at a time.

Carving a shell can be challenging, but the end result makes the effort worthwhile. The Queen Anne scallop shell shown at left adorns the bottom rail of a highboy, decorating it in the style of classical 18th Century furniture.

A SAMPLING OF FAN AND SHELL DESIGNS

Chippendale scallop shell

Queen Anne scallop shell

Louis XIV shell

Chippendale shell

Queen Anne sunburst

Queen Anne fan

Louis XIV shell

Regency flower

Queen Anne shell

CARVING A FAN

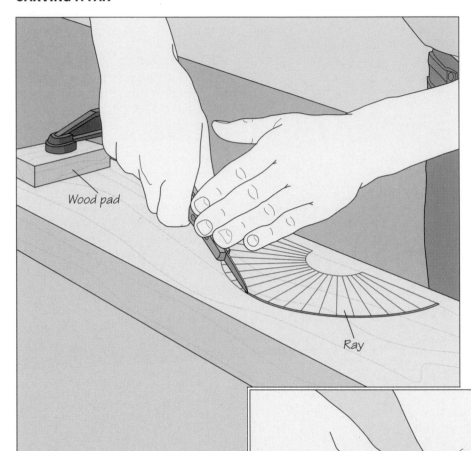

Wood pad

Ray

1 Designing and outlining the fan
Secure your carving block to a work surface, protecting the stock with wood pads. Outline the fan full-size on a sheet of paper, then transfer the design to the carving block *(page 88)*. To design a simple fan, like the one shown at left, start by drawing a semicircle, then use a compass to divide it into equal segments, or rays. The width of the rays is a matter of personal choice and will depend on the size and style of the fan. For this design, you will need an odd number of rays to accommodate the alternating convex and concave ray layout. Once you have transferred the outline to the block, cut lightly around its perimeter with a sharp carving knife *(left)*.

Straight chisel

Convex ray

2 Carving the convex rays
Use a V-parting tool to pare a groove on each of the layout lines dividing the rays. Always cut with the wood grain, reversing your cutting direction if necessary. Then, starting with the first ray at one side of the fan, use a narrow-blade straight chisel to round over the corners of every second ray. These will be the convex rays. Make several cuts on each ray, first creating a faceted surface, then a gently rounded one *(right)*.

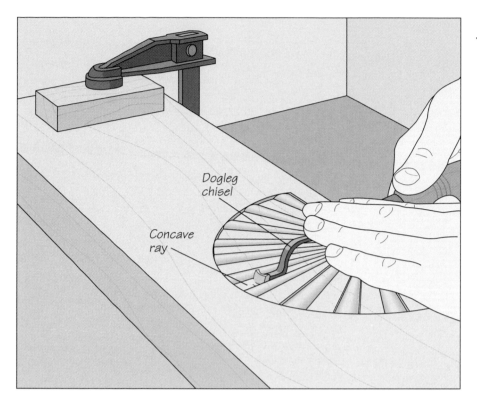

3 Flattening the concave rays
Once you have rounded the convex rays, flatten the concave rays flush with the bottom of the convex rays. Use a narrow straight chisel for the thin portion of the rays and a dogleg chisel for the wider portion near the perimeter of the fan *(left)*.

Dogleg chisel

Concave ray

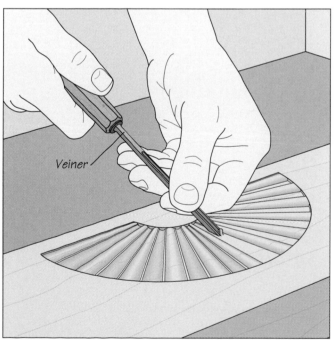

4 Rounding the concave rays
Once all the concave rays have been flattened, round their centers. Use a narrow veiner to carve the narrow sections *(above)*; switch to a No. 5 or 7 gouge for the wider portion of the rays. Leave a 1/16-inch shoulder on each side of each ray.

Veiner

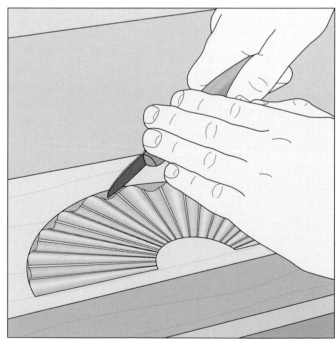

5 Setting in the circumference
Once you have shaped the rays, use a carving knife to trim any remaining waste from the perimeter of the fan *(above)*. Then, starting with 100-grit paper, sand the fan surface with progressively finer grits to give the wood a smooth finish.

CARVING A SHELL

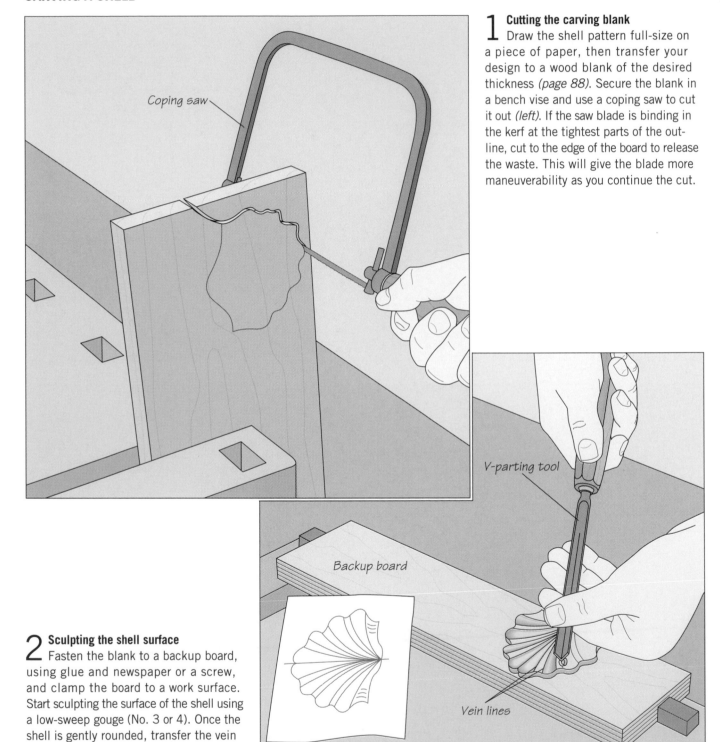

Coping saw

Backup board

V-parting tool

Vein lines

1 Cutting the carving blank

Draw the shell pattern full-size on a piece of paper, then transfer your design to a wood blank of the desired thickness *(page 88)*. Secure the blank in a bench vise and use a coping saw to cut it out *(left)*. If the saw blade is binding in the kerf at the tightest parts of the outline, cut to the edge of the board to release the waste. This will give the blade more maneuverability as you continue the cut.

2 Sculpting the shell surface

Fasten the blank to a backup board, using glue and newspaper or a screw, and clamp the board to a work surface. Start sculpting the surface of the shell using a low-sweep gouge (No. 3 or 4). Once the shell is gently rounded, transfer the vein lines from your pattern to the blank and use a V-parting tool to etch the lines into the wood *(right)*. Make all the cuts in the direction of the wood grain.

3 Rounding the rays

Once all the veins have been cut, use a No. 3 or 4 gouge to round the corners between the vein lines. Start by making the surfaces of all the rays convex (or crowning outward). To finish carving the pattern, carve a concave valley into every second ray with a narrow No. 7 or 8 gouge *(right)*. (For the design shown, the two rays at the center line remain convex.) The result will be that the surfaces of adjacent rays will curve in opposite directions, alternating between convex and concave. Carve carefully at the edges of the blank to avoid tearout.

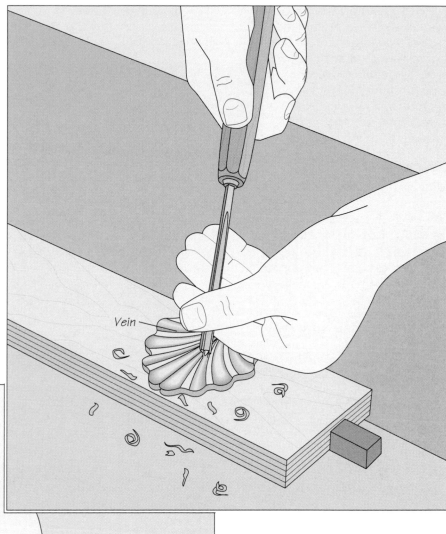

Vein

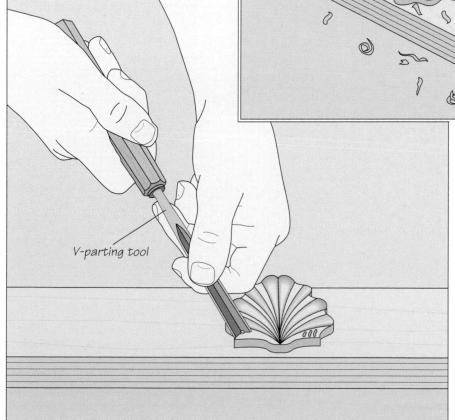

V-parting tool

4 Carving the veins in the wing

Use a V-parting tool to carve the veins in the wings at the bottom of the shell. Make all your cuts with the wood grain; with the workpiece shown at left, this involves carving down from the top of the shell. Once you are satisfied with the shape of the shell, smooth the surface lightly with progressively finer grits of sandpaper, or use a riffler. Remove the workpiece from the backup board.

RELIEF CARVING

Relief carving involves bringing a design into prominence on a piece of wood by removing the background (or waste) surrounding it. The technique has been used for thousands of years to create a diverse range of images, from simple geometric patterns to street scenes and portraits. Relief carvings are of two types. Low reliefs feature a background that is recessed ⅜ inch or less from the work; if the background is recessed more than this, the work appears to stand free of it and the carving is described as high relief. Low relief carving is best for simple designs and patterns; high relief is ide-

al for more detailed work or in cases where the carver wishes to create the illusion of depth.

Based on a classical Greek design, the acanthus leaf has been a favorite with carvers for centuries. The example shown above, produced by Master Carver Adam Thorpe, can be used as a model as you follow the steps detailed below and on the following pages.

Most relief carvings require that you follow these sequence of steps: First, a carving is set in *(step 1)*, then the background is removed *(step 2)*. If you are using either a router fitted with a straight bit or a router plane for this step, the resulting background will have a smooth surface.

It is common practice to remove the background with a gouge; this will leave a slightly rough surface that will stand in contrast to the finished carving. Once the background is completed, the carving is rough-shaped, or bosted in *(step 3)*, then modeled to finished quality and undercut *(steps 4 and 5)*.

CARVING AN ACANTHUS LEAF

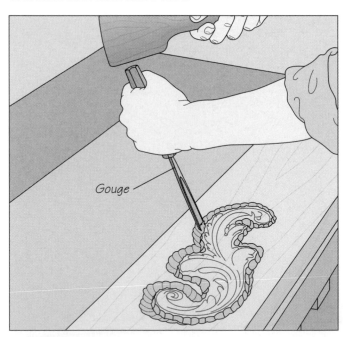

1 Setting in the pattern
Draw your pattern full-size on a piece of paper, then transfer the design to your carving block *(page 88)*. Each of the vein lines on the leaves or valleys between leaves should be represented by a pattern line. Clamp the board to a work surface and begin setting in the carving. Make a series of cuts around the outline using a V-parting tool, striking the tool with a mallet, if necessary. The resulting groove should begin ¼ inch outside the pattern; steer clear of any fine details for now. Next, use a gouge of relatively

shallow sweep (No. 3 or 5) with a mallet to widen the groove, angling the gouge to carve from the outside in *(above, left)*. When the groove is roughed in, carve to the marked outline; at each point, use a gouge whose sweep matches the curve of the design. Also use a mallet to ensure that the outside edges of the carving are vertical *(above, right)*. Continue the entire process, widening the groove and flattening the edges of the carving, until you have set in the background to the desired depth.

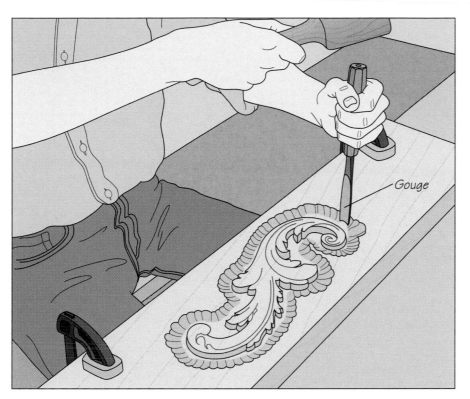

Gouge

2 Removing the background

When the carving is set in, use a mallet and a straight gouge with a shallow sweep to remove the background. In the example shown here, the background will be removed from the entire surface of the workpiece. Starting at one end of the carving, hold the chisel vertically and perpendicular to the wood grain, and tap it with a mallet to break out a chip of waste wood *(left)*. Move the tool laterally and back about ¼ inch, then make the next cut. Continue until you have reached the end of the workpiece and cut away the background to the required depth. Repeat at the other end of the carving and along the sides. Use a shallow-sweep gouge, holding the tool horizontally, to finish the background to the desired smoothness.

3 Bosting in the carving

Now you are ready to rough out the basic shape of the carving, a process called bosting in. First, use a V-parting tool with a mallet to carve the valleys between the leaves and the veins within them to the desired depth. These details are represented by pattern lines. Start at one end of each line and carve along its length. In difficult grain, you may need to stop partway through a cut and complete it from the other end of the line. In hard stock, use a mallet to tap the tool *(right)*. Next, round off the sharp corners on the outside and inside of the carving to their rough shape. For the outside curves of the leaf, use a gouge of shallow sweep to carve in broad sweeps around the curves. Rough out the inside edges using a gouge with a deep curvature, carving down from the top *(inset)*. Do not try to add detail or carve perfectly smooth contours at this point. The idea is simply to rough out the general shape of the work.

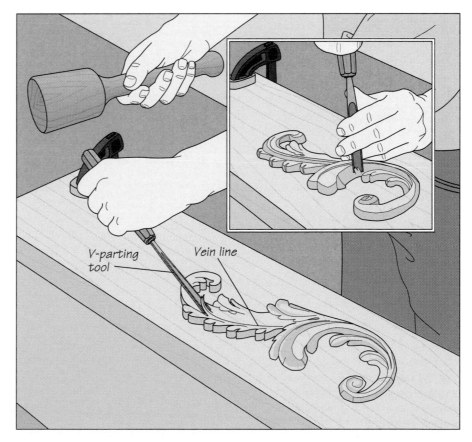

V-parting tool

Vein line

4 Carving the piping

When the work is rough-shaped, you can begin to carve the details, starting with the pipings and the eyes. Pipings are raised tubular segments created when adjacent sections are indented to suggest a fold in the leaf. Eyes (visible in the illustration below) are teardrop-shaped holes which simulate a fold between two overlapping leaves. Before carving the pipings and eyes, transfer any lines you may need from the pattern onto the workpiece. For the pipings, use a veiner to carve the valleys adjoining them. Work in the direction of the the grain, using only hand pressure *(right)*. Then use a narrow No. 5 gouge to smooth the edges of the pipings to the desired shape. Once the pipings are carved, cut the eyes. Use the veiner, but cut vertically, tapping the tool with a mallet.

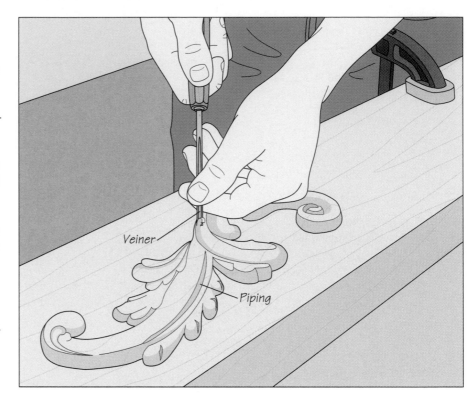

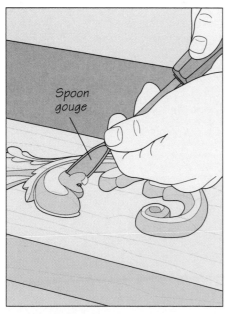

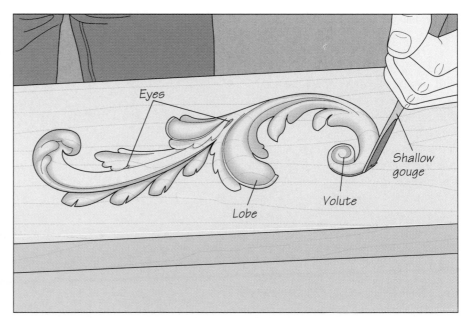

5 Modeling the curves

Once you have completed the pipings and eyes, model the leaf. To round over the outside curves, use a shallow gouge and hold the tool convex-side down; use a spoon gouge with a deep curvature for the sharp interior curves *(above, left)*. All your cuts should be long and sweeping, made with the grain. Next, round over the lobes at the ends of the leaves; they should seem to droop naturally. The volute at the other end of the leaf should be stepped—high in the center and spiraling down into the body of the leaf. Continue modeling until you are satisfied with the shape of the work. Then, use a shallow gouge to undercut the carving. Remove ⅛ inch of wood from the base of its edges, creating a shadow around the workpiece *(above, right)*.

LINENFOLD PANELS

Designed to duplicate in wood the folds of an altar cloth, the linenfold panel is one of the enduring styles of relief carving. Brought to England from continental Europe in the 15th Century, it caught on rapidly and today can be found on the walls of houses and churches, as well as on beds, cabinets, and chests.

Carving linenfold involves two basic steps: First, the undulations of the folds are carved, then the ends are sculpted. The folds were traditionally cut with straight and curved hand planes that are extremely difficult to find today. The following pages demonstrate two alternative modern methods for producing the folds, one using a table saw *(page 102)* and a second using the saw along with gouges *(page 103)*. The ends are sculpt-ed with an assortment of carving tools *(page 104)*.

There are hundreds of traditional linenfold patterns. In fact, wood-carvers covering a room with linenfold in centuries past would alter the design of each panel slightly. A sampling of the more common designs is shown below.

The linenfold panel shown above, produced by a student at the school of Master Carver Ian Agrell, features the undulating folds and sculpted lacework that distinguish this centuries-old design.

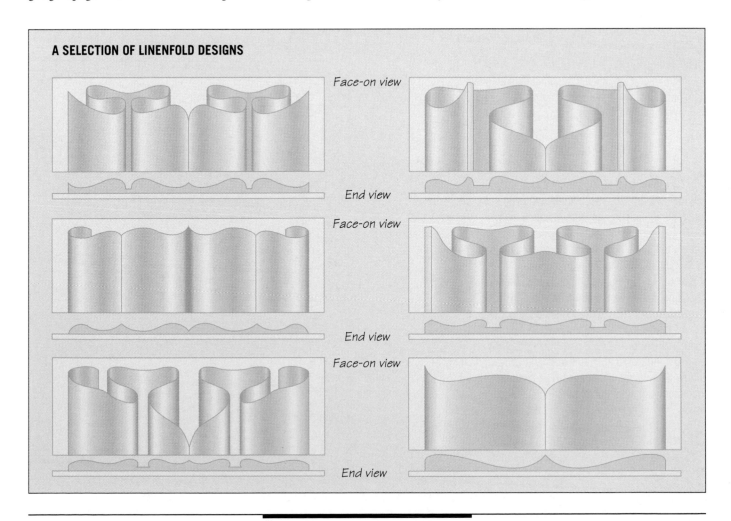

A SELECTION OF LINENFOLD DESIGNS

Face-on view

End view

Face-on view

End view

Face-on view

End view

CUTTING THE FOLDS ON THE TABLE SAW

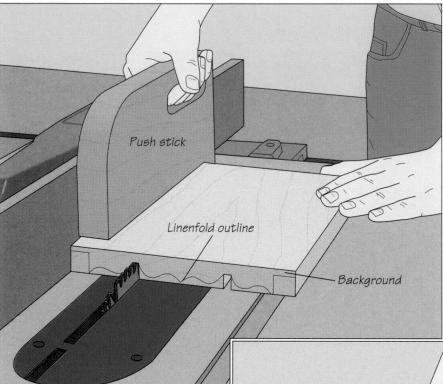

Push stick

Linenfold outline

Background

1 Cutting the deep grooves
Outline the linenfold pattern on both ends of your panel; also outline the background on its inside face. Start by cutting the deep grooves, as shown at left, then shape the folds *(step 2)* and saw away the background *(step 3)*. To cut the grooves, align one with the blade, butt the rip fence against the edge of the panel, and adjust the blade depth. Pressing the panel against the fence, use a push stick to feed the workpiece. For a wide groove, you may need to make more than one pass. For the pattern shown, cut the second groove by rotating the workpiece 180° and make a second pass *(left)*.

2 Shaping the folds
The folds are shaped on the saw with a molding head fitted with the appropriate cutters. Since the contours on either side of the panel are mirror images of each other, the same cutter can be used to make both cuts—provided the workpiece is rotated 180° between passes. For each cut, use a molding cutter with the appropriate profile for one section of the outline. Position the panel face-down on the saw table in front of the cutter and adjust the cutting height to align the cutter with the marked outline. Then lower the cutterhead and make a pass that is no deeper than ⅛ inch, feeding the stock with a push stick as in step 1. Reverse the board and repeat the cut on the other side. Make as many passes as necessary, raising the cutting height ⅛ inch at a time. Use the same technique to shape the other sections of the panel *(right)*.

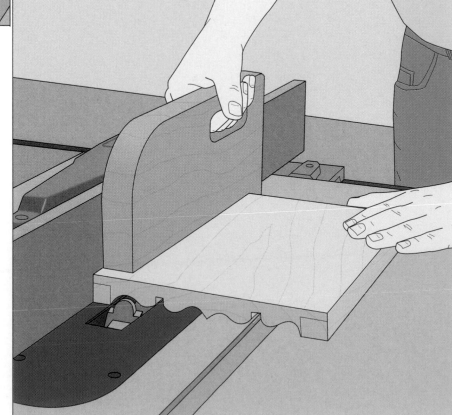

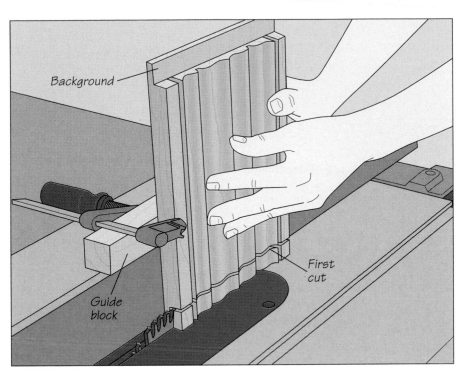

Background

Guide block

First cut

3 Cutting the background

Once the contours of the panel are cut, remove the molding cutterhead and install a crosscut blade on the table saw. Cut away the background in two steps, first notching the inside face of the panel, then feeding it into the blade on end and on edge. To make the first cuts, set the blade height to the depth of the background and feed the panel, inside-face down, along the marked lines. Now hold the panel end-up on the saw table and align the blade with the bottom of the kerfs cut in the panel face. Clamp a guide block to the panel to ride along the top of the rip fence and, keeping the panel flush against the fence, feed it on end to remove one section of the background. Turn the workpiece over to cut the background at the other end *(left)*. Repeat the process to remove the background from the edges.

CARVING THE FOLDS BY HAND

Shaping the folds

To shape the folds of a linenfold panel by hand, you first need to cut any deep grooves *(page 102)* and remove the background *(step above)* on the table saw, as shown in the previous section. Then clamp the panel to a work surface so you have access to one side and chip away at the waste in the folds using gouges with sweeps that match the desired contours. Work in a relatively straight line from one end of the panel to the other, tapping the tool with a mallet *(right)*. Once the contours are rough-shaped, give them a final shaping, working the gouge with hand pressure only. Reposition the clamps to work the other side of the panel.

Gouge

CARVING THE ENDS

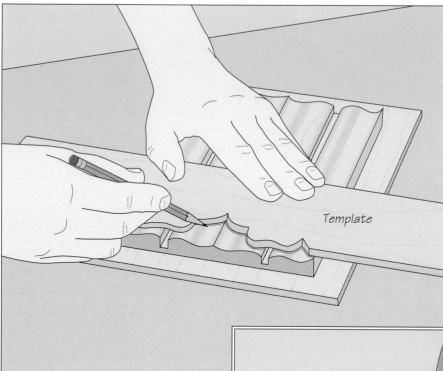

Template

1 Outlining the end folds
Once the folds on the main part of the panel are done, you can carve the end folds. Copy your design full-size onto a piece of paper, and then transfer it to the panel; or, you can make a template, as shown at left. For the template, trace your design on a board and cut it out using a band saw or saber saw. Then, hold the template across the top end of the panel and use a sharp pencil to trace the outline of the end folds on the workpiece *(left)*.

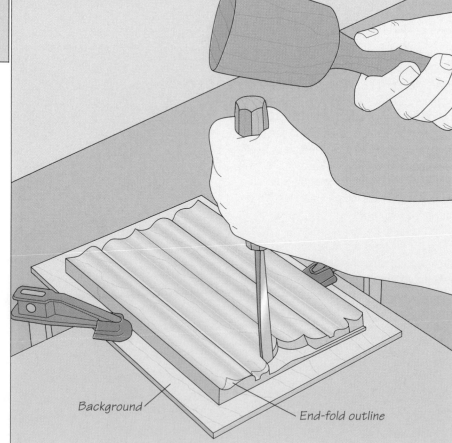

Background

End-fold outline

2 Setting in the end-fold pattern
The end-fold pattern is set in with gouges and chisels. The ends are defined first, then the inner folds are set in and sculpted. To define the ends, clamp the panel to a work surface and work from one edge of the panel to the other to chop away the waste. For each cut, hold a gouge or a V-tool with the appropriate curve vertically on the outline and strike the handle with a mallet *(right)*. Cut down to within ⅛ inch of the background. (This protects the background for now, but the waste will be removed later in step 4.)

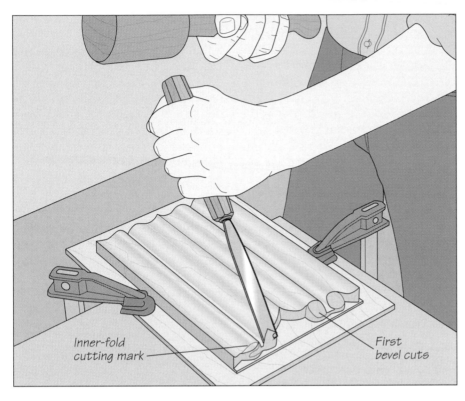

3 Setting in the inner folds
Mark the inner folds on the end of the panel with a pencil. Then rough in the transition from the inside layer of the linen to the outside layer by making bevel cuts with a chisel. The cuts should all start at the marked cutting line and slope downward to within about ¼ inch of the background. For each cut, tap the chisel with a mallet, working from one side of the panel to the other *(left)*.

Inner-fold cutting mark

First bevel cuts

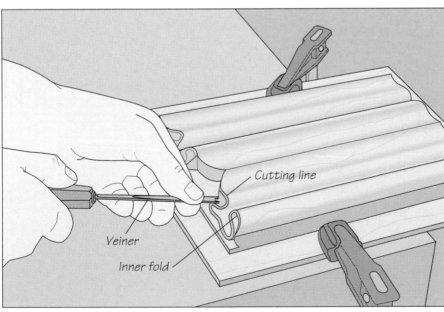

Cutting line

Veiner

Inner fold

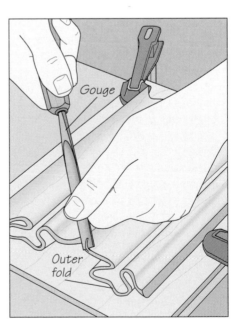

Gouge

Outer fold

4 Sculpting the ends
Once all the bevel cuts are made, mark the ends of the folds on the beveled end of the panel. Then begin sculpting the panel's end with a 60° V-parting tool, carving along the outline of the folds. Next, use a narrow veiner to remove waste from between the inner and outer folds, holding the tool horizontally *(above, left)*. Undercut the folds slightly, leaving them about ⅛ inch thick; use the veiner for the inner folds and a gouge of moderate sweep for the outer folds. At the same time, remove the last of the waste from the background you left in step 1. Finally, use the gouge to bevel the ends of the folds so they will catch the light *(above, right)*. Sand any rough spots with fine sandpaper, making sure not to round over any edges created by the chisels.

CARVING IN THE ROUND

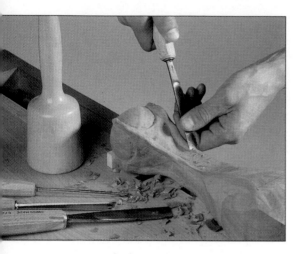

Once the lower portion of the claw-and-ball is carved, a shallow gouge is used to smooth the transition from the claw to the ankle of the cabriole leg before final sanding.

Carving in the round, or 3-D carving, differs in one obvious way from the other carving techniques shown in this chapter: The project must be conceived and worked on from all sides. Although there are no absolute rules that govern carving in the round, your work will benefit from a methodical approach. Whether your piece is a bust, a wildlife carving, or a design element on a piece of furniture like the claw-and-ball foot shown in the photo at left, you should undertake a careful study of the project before beginning, including sketching front and side views. These can be transferred to the carving block, allowing you to band saw your piece to an accurately proportioned blank.

The claw-and-ball foot is one of the most common examples of carving in the round for furniture, and is a good starting point for 3-D work. The design is thought to have been adapted from a traditional Chinese motif depicting a dragon's claw protecting a sacred pearl, representing wisdom and purity. The design was brought to England from China in the 16th Century, and rose to prominence in the 18th Century as the favorite decoration for the feet of cabriole legs. The style remains popular on reproduction pieces today.

The steps shown below and on the following pages will enable you to create a traditional claw-and-ball. The dimensions are up to you; these and many other design elements are a matter of personal choice, depending on the piece of furniture being built and the effect you desire.

CARVING A CLAW-AND-BALL FOOT

1 Rough-shaping the blank

Cut a cabriole leg to the shape shown in step 2 on page 107, making sure the foot blank is larger than the finished claw-and-ball will be. The first step is to cut away a wedge from each side claw. The locations of these cuts are represented by the red lines in the end-view illustration of the leg *(inset)*. The remaining waste, represented by the shaded gray areas, is removed in steps 2 through 7. To start, outline the wedge cuts on the top and bottom of the foot and secure the leg flat on a work surface. Then use a straight chisel with a mallet to cut away the wedges from the side claws *(right)*. Cut to the marked line, then turn the leg over and repeat the cut on the other side.

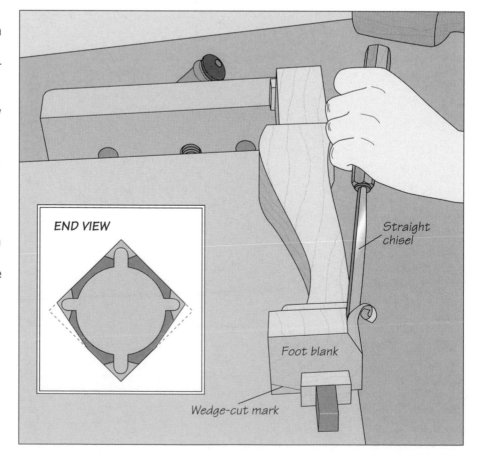

END VIEW

Straight chisel

Foot blank

Wedge-cut mark

2 Marking the claws

Use a sharp pencil to outline the claws. Holding the leg firmly in one hand, draw guidelines on both sides of each corner of the foot, about ¼ inch from the edge. Use your fingers as a guide, running it along the adjoining side of the leg while you draw the line. Then extend the lines to the ankle *(right)*.

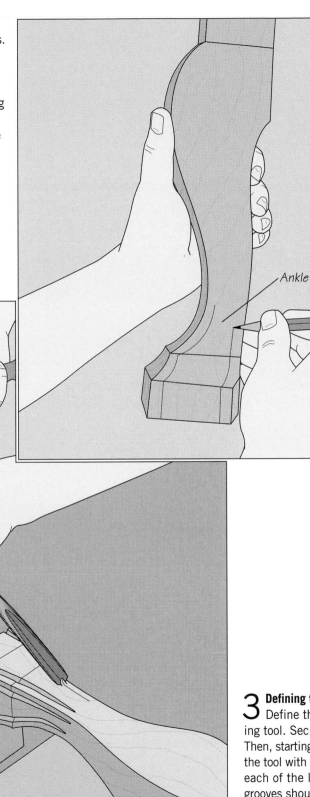

3 Defining the claws

Define the claws using a 60° V-parting tool. Secure the leg to a work surface. Then, starting at the bottom of the foot, tap the tool with a mallet to cut a groove along each of the lines marked in step 2. The grooves should begin at the full thickness of the claw, but become gradually shallower as they extend onto the ankle *(left)*.

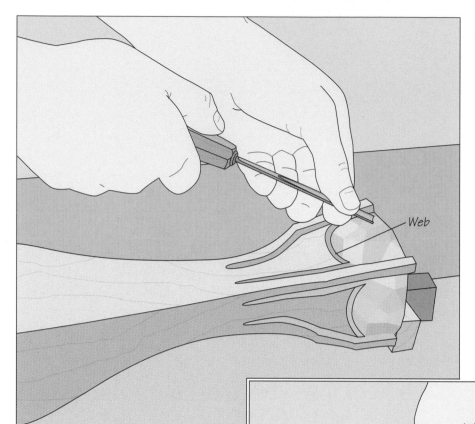

4 **Roughing out the ball**
Once the claws are roughly formed, begin shaping the ball. First define its top edge—where the ball will meet the web—using gouges with the appropriate sweeps. Make each of these cuts across the grain by holding the tool vertically and tapping it with a mallet. Next, use a shallow-sweep gouge to round the ball *(left)*. Work patiently; do not try to clear away too much waste with a single cut. Repeat the process on each side of the foot, repositioning the leg in the bench dogs or clamps as necessary.

5 **Detailing the claws**
With the claw-and-ball roughed in, carve the details on the claws using narrow, shallow-sweep gouges. The claws should slope down smoothly from the ankle to the knuckles, and the thickness of the claws should conform to the curvature of the ball. Once you are satisfied with the shape of the claws, carve the nails and cuticles. Use a narrow gouge of the appropriate sweep to define the cuticle, cutting across the grain. Then carve the nail, sloping in toward the ball at the bottom of the foot *(right)*. As a general rule, the cuticle should be located about ½ inch from the bottom of the foot with the nail carved on it, tapering to ⅛ inch high and wide at the bottom.

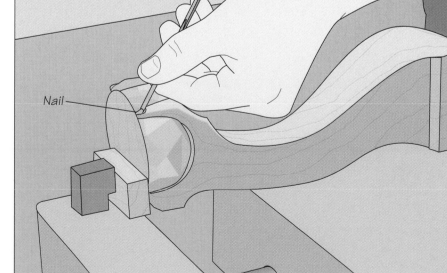

6 Defining the webbing

Once the claws are completed, choose a gouge with a sweep that matches the contours of the web to better define the transition between the ball and the web. Starting on one side of the foot, tap the tool with a mallet to cut around the top of the ball *(right)*. Then, use a shallow-sweep gouge to give the ball a final shaping. Repeat the cuts on each side of the foot.

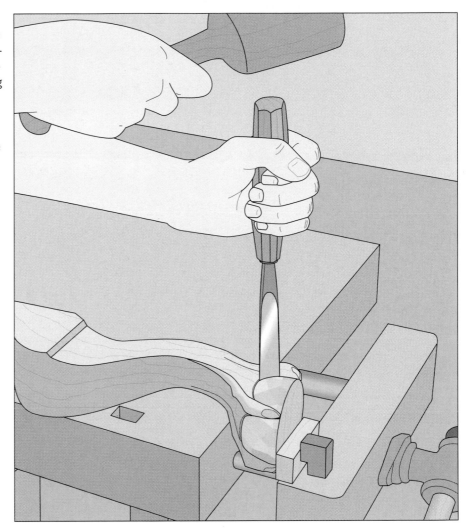

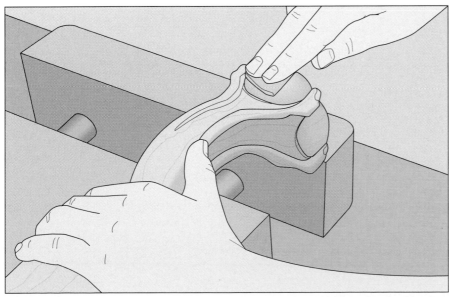

7 Smoothing the claw-and-ball

Use sandpaper to finish the claw-and-ball *(left)*. For a smooth finish, use progressively finer grits. To reach the tight corners between the claws and the webbing, fold the paper and sand with an edge. If you wish, leave some of the tool marks visible.

VENEER, INLAY, AND MARQUETRY

At least since the time of Egypt's Pharaohs, craftsmen have relied on veneering, inlaying, and marquetry to embellish furniture and create effects often unattainable with solid wood. All involve overlaying or inlaying a workpiece with very thin pieces of wood. But each has a unique use. Veneer can transform a plain wood surface into a stunning arrangement of color and grain. Inlay banding is especially effective for accenting a design element. In marquetry, where woodworking meets pictorial art, wood is the medium for creating portraits, landscapes, and abstract patterns.

One object of veneering is to conceal a relatively unattractive wood surface—usually a tabletop or a carcase panel made of plywood or low-grade lumber—with a thin covering of a more appealing species. A sampling of commonly available veneer woods is shown beginning on page 112. But veneering should not be thought of only as a less expensive way of disguising a plain wood. It is that, but many woodworkers use veneer for stability, because it permits them to use plywood core stock, which is less prone to shrinking and warping than solid wood.

Veneering has passed in and out of favor throughout history, the result of changing attitudes toward craftsmanship and advances in technology. Today, its popularity stems in part from the increasing scarcity of exotic woods; some varieties are now available only in veneer form. As more woodworkers

A fret saw is used with a bird's-mouth table to cut veneer for marquetry. The table features a V-cutout to accommodate the saw. For the cut shown above, the table is shimmed to create a bevel on the cut edges, ensuring seamless joints between the pieces of veneer.

search for ways to help preserve the world's valuable forests while continuing to use exotic woods, veneers offer a solution to their dilemma. A 10-foot-long 2-by-12 plank contains 20 board feet of lumber; the same piece will yield 600 square feet of veneer.

With the matching techniques shown on page 123, you can arrange veneers on a workpiece to take maximum advantage of their wood grain. Veneering also allows you to use beautiful but unstable wood cuts like burl and crotch, which are nearly impossible to work in solid form. See pages 120 and 121 for an inventory of veneering tools. Procedures for making and applying veneer begin on page 122.

Inlaying is the process of setting a strip of contrasting material into a recess cut in the surface of a workpiece. Inlay materials range from simple strips of exotic wood or metal to elaborate designs consisting of several veneers. Inlaying techniques are shown starting on page 134.

Marquetry is the art of "painting" with veneer. The veneers available cover the standard color palette, but some woodworkers use dyes to broaden their choices. For a novice, a commercial marquetry kit *(page 132)* offers the easiest way to get started. These kits work like paint-by-numbers sets. They include a copy of the finished design, the appropriate veneers, and detailed instructions.

A shop-made veneer press like the one shown at left is ideal for bonding veneer to core stock. Once the glue is applied and the veneer is set in place, the veneer and substrate are sandwiched between a pair of plywood cauls. The press screws are then tightened to hold the veneer in place while the adhesive dries. A sheet of wax paper protects the veneer and prevents it from adhering to the upper caul.

GALLERY OF VENEERS

Veneers are thin layers of wood sliced or sawn from the highest quality logs of selected domestic and exotic hardwoods. There are thousands of hardwood species worldwide; about 200 species are available in veneer in signif-icant quantities. The visual diversity of these woods is astonishing. Some species, like holly and pearwood, are virtually unfigured; others, like bird's-eye maple or fiddleback mahogany, are distinctly patterned. To some extent, the variation depends on where in the tree the veneer originated and how it was cut or sliced. The illustrations and chart on pages 118 and 119 explain this more fully.

Throughout the history of wood-working, individual veneer species have

Bubinga
Sometimes called African rosewood, bubinga has a dark purple color. Figured wood typically possesses a bee's wing or black mottle. When rotary cut, the veneer possesses a striking flame figure, highly valued for cabinetry. On the American market, bubinga is more common as lumber than veneer. Choice flitches can often be obtained, but at fairly high cost.

Ebony, macassar
Native to southeast Asia, macassar is the principal ebony in the North American veneer market. Its color is a striking dark brown to black with lightbrown streaks. Used mainly in wall paneling and for decorative inlay work, the wood is occasionally avail-able as veneer but is expensive.

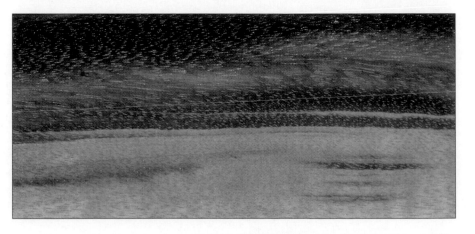

Goncalo alves
This straw-colored wood's deep brown and black streaks bear a resemblance to macassar ebony and rosewood. This species extends from Brazil to Mexico. Although it is relatively plentiful, not all logs contain the highly figured wood used in cabinetmaking. It is usu-ally quarter-sliced. Goncalo alves is relatively expensive, even as veneer.

come in and out of fashion. During the 1950s and 1960s, cherry, walnut, mahogany, and oak were the most prized veneers. In the decades since, species like pecan and red oak have become increasingly popular.

The style of furniture often determines which species of veneer a cabinetmaker will select for his project. For example, colonial American furniture is usually made from walnut, cherry, maple, or pine. The rococo styles of the Louis XV period in the mid-1700s feature kingwood, purpleheart, tulipwood, and rosewood.

The following pages showcase a selection of veneers, both domestic and exotic, common and uncommon.

Holly
Though its sources include parts of Europe and western Asia, most usable holly grows in a limited range in Tennessee and Kentucky. It is a white wood with extremely close grain and little or no visible figure. As such, it is highly valued for inlay work and is often dyed black to resemble ebony. Supplies of holly are rapidly diminishing, however, and it is becoming rare as veneer.

Lacewood, Australian
Often used interchangeably with silky oak, lacewood possesses a distinctive flake figure that varies in intensity from flitch to flitch. While the lumber bears a certain resemblance to oak's reddish-brown color, lacewood has a far more striking figure when quartersawn. It is rare and fairly expensive as veneer.

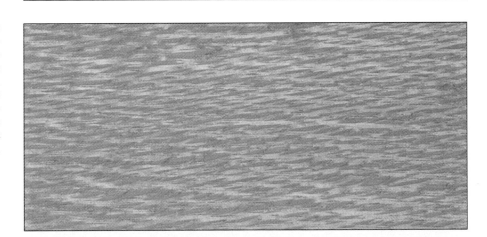

Mahogany, fiddleback
This prized veneer can be produced from any one of the three primary species of mahogany: African, tropical American, and Cuban. Fiddleback is but one of many figures generated by this celebrated timber. Mottles, broken stripes, crotches, and swirls are also available.

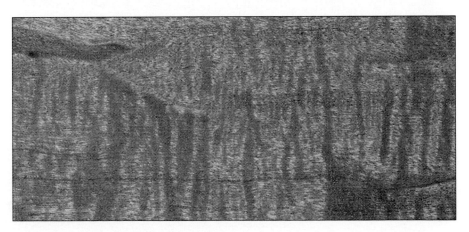

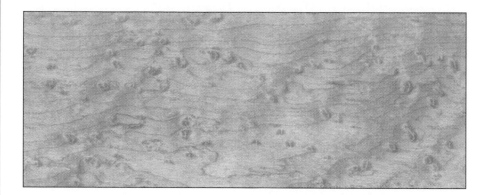

Maple, bird's-eye
Cut from irregularly grained hard maple logs, bird's-eye veneer is harvested primarily from trees growing in Michigan's Upper Peninsula. The origin of the figure is uncertain, but it is believed to be caused by stress —a deprivation or a limitation of some important nutrient.

Maple, quilted
Quilt figure is found in both hard and soft maple timber, and is highly valued for cabinetwork when cut into veneer. The primary source of quilted maple is Oregon, or big-leaf, maple which grows along the Pacific coast of North America. High-quality quilted maple veneer is rare and quite expensive.

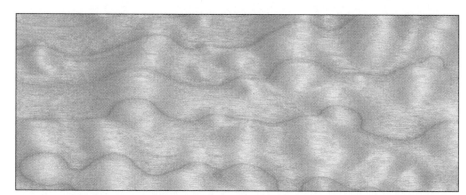

Oak, English brown
Originating from the same two species as European oak, English oak is distinguished by dark or black markings in its heartwood, caused by a fungus. The timber occasionally produces stunning burls, swirls, and an attractive flake figure, all highly prized as veneer. It is available in limited quantities and is very costly.

Oak, white
One of the most widely used woods in the world, white oak is usually rift-cut or flat-cut into veneer for plywood and fine cabinetry applications. It features a characteristic straight grain and light tan to yellowish color. White oak grows throughout the United States and Canada. It occasionally produces burls, swirls, and crotch veneers.

Osage orange

Sometimes known as bowwood, this greenish-yellow timber grows in the midwestern United States. It is rarely cut into solid lumber, but selected logs are sliced into a veneer valued for its mottled figure.

Padauk

Growing through Central Africa, this lesser-known padauk is more readily available than its famed cousin from the Andaman Islands. It is a deep red to purple-brown wood, and yields stunning veneers. Like Andaman padauk, African padauk possesses a broken stripe, often blended with a bee's wing mottled figure when it is quarter-sliced.

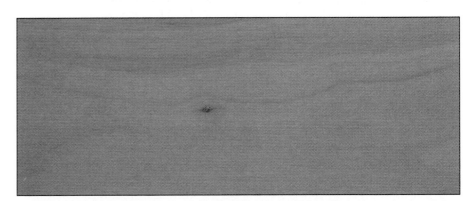

Pear

Most of the pearwood on the market comes from Europe's alpine region. The timber yields a close-grained veneer with fine, virtually imperceptible pores. Pear veneer is available in small sizes and is relatively expensive. It is commonly dyed black to resemble ebony for fine inlay work.

Purpleheart

Also known as amaranth, purpleheart veneer vividly deserves its name. Its rich purple color is valued for inlays, panels, and marquetry. The tree itself is commonly found in Central and South America. As veneer, purpleheart is readily available but somewhat expensive.

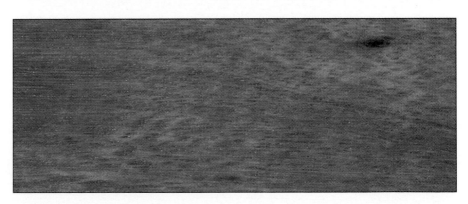

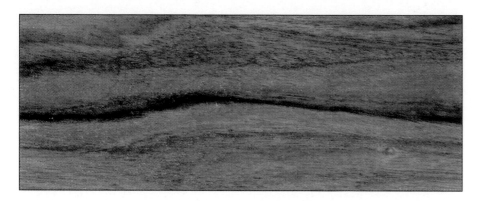

Rosewood, Honduras
With its characteristic pinkish-brown to purple coloring with dark, irregular grain lines, Honduras rosewood is lighter in color than most other rosewoods. It can be highly figured. Traditionally less important to the American market, this species may now see increased use as veneer with the recent trade ban on Brazilian rosewood.

Sycamore
The sycamore is a huge tree, often growing 200 feet or higher. It is readily available in veneer form, typically quarter-sliced or rotary cut, although it is also prized as solid lumber for drawer sides. When quarter-sliced, the veneer possesses an attractive flake figure, similar to Australian lacewood.

Teak
Exceptionally valuable in solid form, teak veneer is most commonly used for interior paneling, fine furniture, and cabinetwork when it is cut into veneer. Depending on the area of growth, it varies in color from straw to darker brown, and occasionally has subtle darker stripes. Teak veneer remains in fairly good supply on the American market, but it is fairly expensive.

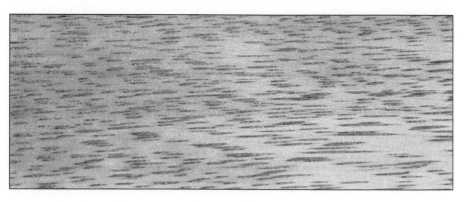

Tornillo
Relatively new to the United States market, tornillo is an attractive and common tropical hardwood. It is used as a mahogany substitute, although tornillo is denser and grainier. Its heartwood, of primary importance to the veneer market, combines light brown and pink coloring with straight to irregular grain.

Tulipwood

Tulipwood comes from a small tree that, like other rosewoods, requires centuries to develop its rich coloring. Rarely available in solid form, tulipwood yields a stunning veneer, full of yellow, rose violet, and darker markings. It is relatively difficult to obtain, and is used primarily for fine inlay work and trim.

Walnut, black

Ranging in color from light gray to dark brown, walnut is the principal American veneer. It is normally flat-cut, although butt, burl, and crotch veneers are occasionally available. Export to Europe and Japan has reduced domestic supply, but black walnut veneer is still readily available.

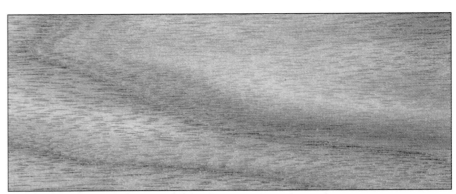

Wenge

A distinct deep brown and black wood, wenge is not readily available as veneer. This is a result of both the rarity of the lumber and the difficulty in slicing this hard, coarse-textured wood. The best wenge veneer is often enhanced by white streaks of parenchyma, a tree tissue involved in food storage. Wenge is used in fine cabinetry and paneling.

Zebrawood

Cut from two species of large trees mainly found in Cameroon and Gabon, West Africa, this veneer exhibits distinct straw-colored and dark brown stripes. It is most often quarter-sliced. Zebrawood veneer is readily available, relatively expensive, and extremely fragile.

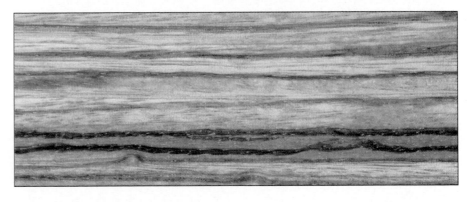

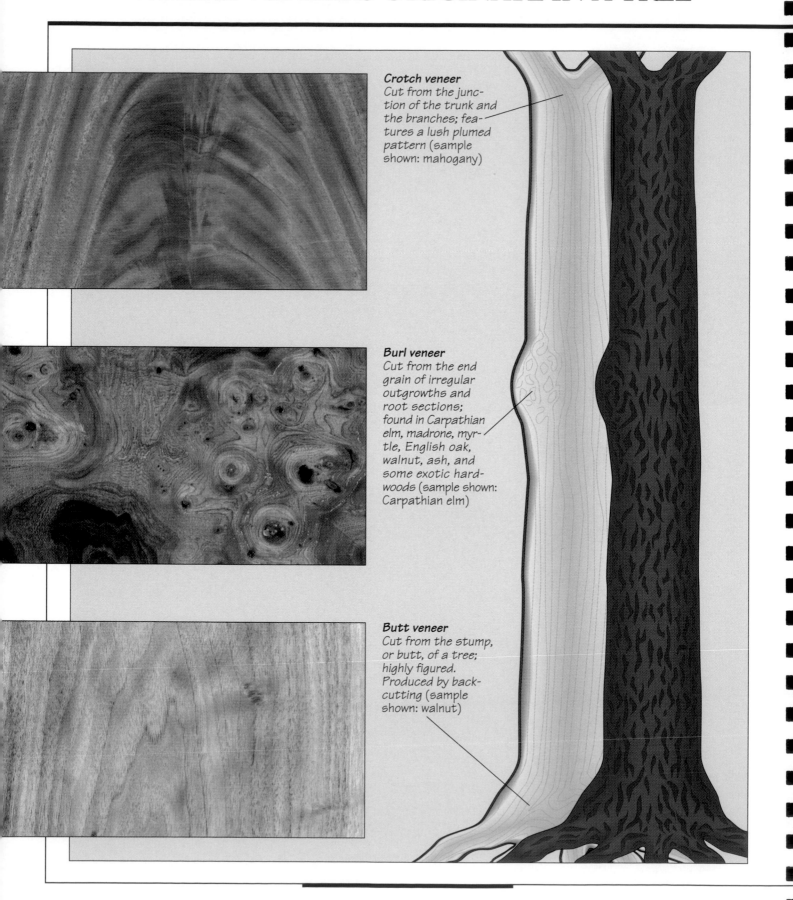

Crotch veneer
Cut from the junction of the trunk and the branches; features a lush plumed pattern (sample shown: mahogany)

Burl veneer
Cut from the end grain of irregular outgrowths and root sections; found in Carpathian elm, madrone, myrtle, English oak, walnut, ash, and some exotic hardwoods (sample shown: Carpathian elm)

Butt veneer
Cut from the stump, or butt, of a tree; highly figured. Produced by back-cutting (sample shown: walnut)

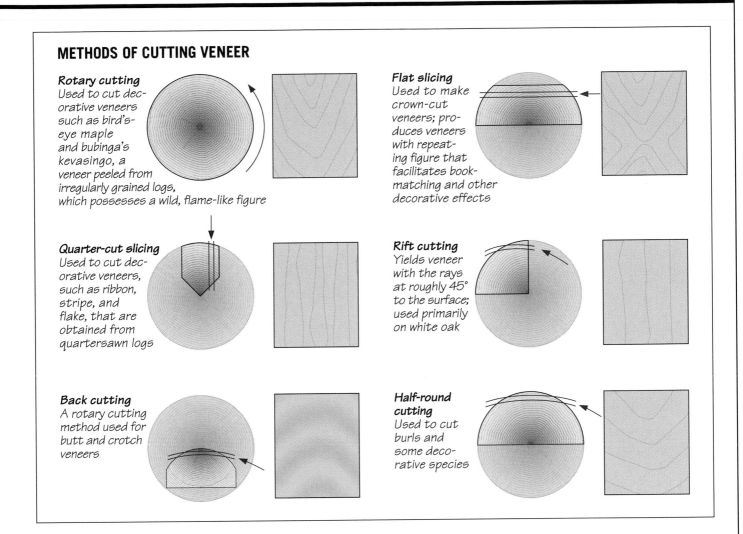

METHODS OF CUTTING VENEER

Rotary cutting
Used to cut decorative veneers such as bird's-eye maple and bubinga's kevasingo, a veneer peeled from irregularly grained logs, which possesses a wild, flame-like figure

Flat slicing
Used to make crown-cut veneers; produces veneers with repeating figure that facilitates bookmatching and other decorative effects

Quarter-cut slicing
Used to cut decorative veneers, such as ribbon, stripe, and flake, that are obtained from quartersawn logs

Rift cutting
Yields veneer with the rays at roughly 45° to the surface; used primarily on white oak

Back cutting
A rotary cutting method used for butt and crotch veneers

Half-round cutting
Used to cut burls and some decorative species

VENEER TYPES AND SIZES

VENEER TYPE	SIZES	SOME AVAILABLE SPECIES
Rotary cut	Length up to 10 feet; width from 8 to 36 inches	Bird's-eye maple, bubinga, Douglas-fir
Quarter-cut	Length 3 to 16 feet; width from 3 to 12 inches	Avodire, mahogany, oak, Queensland maple, sapele, satinwood, zebrawood
Butt	Irregular dimensions. Sheet sizes vary from 10 x 36 to 18 x 54 inches; average sheet size 12 x 36 inches	Maple, walnut
Crotch	Length from 18 to 54 inches; width from 10 to 24 inches. Average sheet size 12 x 36 inches	Amburana, English oak, mahogany, walnut
Flat-sliced	Length 3 to 16 feet; width from 4 to 24 inches	Ash, Brazilian rosewood, cherry, maple, oak, teak
Burl	Irregular dimensions. Sheet sizes vary from 8 x 10 to 18 x 54 inches; average sheet size 16 x 24 inches	Carpathian elm, English oak, madrone, myrtle, padauk, redwood, thuya, walnut

AN INVENTORY OF VENEERING TOOLS

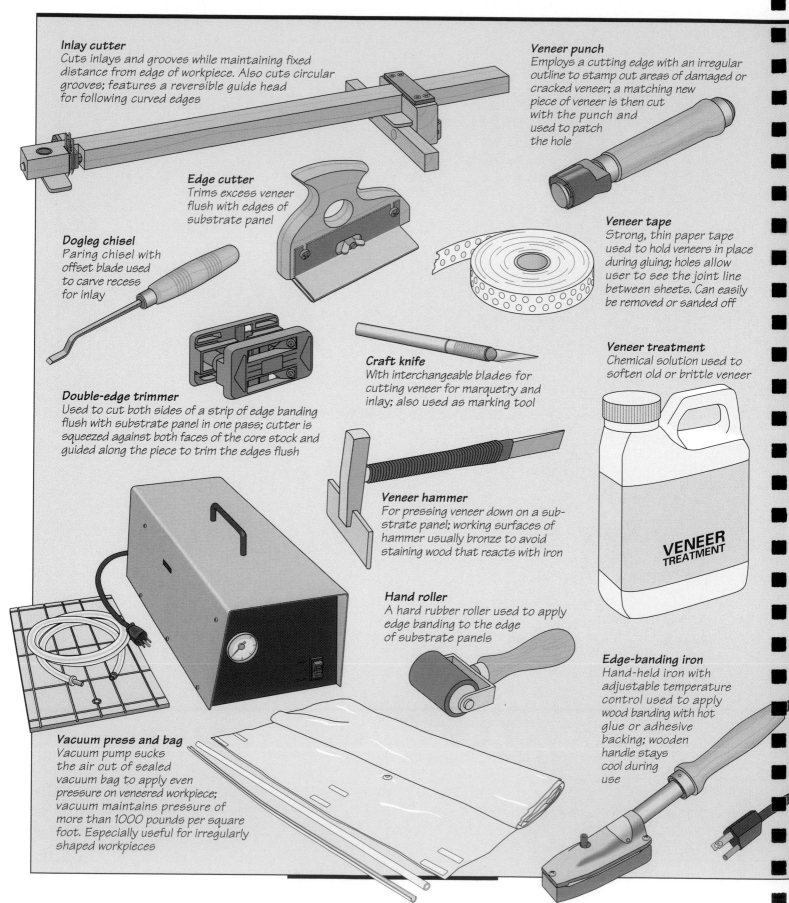

Inlay cutter
Cuts inlays and grooves while maintaining fixed distance from edge of workpiece. Also cuts circular grooves; features a reversible guide head for following curved edges

Edge cutter
Trims excess veneer flush with edges of substrate panel

Dogleg chisel
Paring chisel with offset blade used to carve recess for inlay

Double-edge trimmer
Used to cut both sides of a strip of edge banding flush with substrate panel in one pass; cutter is squeezed against both faces of the core stock and guided along the piece to trim the edges flush

Craft knife
With interchangeable blades for cutting veneer for marquetry and inlay; also used as marking tool

Veneer hammer
For pressing veneer down on a substrate panel; working surfaces of hammer usually bronze to avoid staining wood that reacts with iron

Hand roller
A hard rubber roller used to apply edge banding to the edge of substrate panels

Vacuum press and bag
Vacuum pump sucks the air out of sealed vacuum bag to apply even pressure on veneered workpiece; vacuum maintains pressure of more than 1000 pounds per square foot. Especially useful for irregularly shaped workpieces

Veneer punch
Employs a cutting edge with an irregular outline to stamp out areas of damaged or cracked veneer; a matching new piece of veneer is then cut with the punch and used to patch the hole

Veneer tape
Strong, thin paper tape used to hold veneers in place during gluing; holes allow user to see the joint line between sheets. Can easily be removed or sanded off

Veneer treatment
Chemical solution used to soften old or brittle veneer

VENEER TREATMENT

Edge-banding iron
Hand-held iron with adjustable temperature control used to apply wood banding with hot glue or adhesive backing; wooden handle stays cool during use

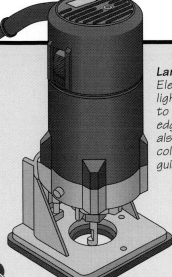

Laminate edge trimmer
Electrically powered light-weight router used to trim veneer flush with edge of substrate panel; also functions as a 1/4-inch-collet router that can be guided with one hand

Veneer nails
Used to hold matched veneer leaves together until tape is applied; fine tips divide wood fibers instead of severing them

Needle-point glue injector
Syringe-type glue applicator with 1 1/4-inch-long needle for applying glue in hard-to-reach areas

Fret saw
Bow-type saw with fine blade 5 to 6 inches long, used to cut curved shapes in thin wood, plywood, and veneer; commonly used for marquetry

Plastic glue injectors
Used for injecting glue into restricted spaces

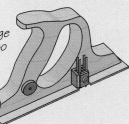

Veneer saw
Used for trimming and cutting veneer; its curved blade, offset handle, and thin, sharp-tipped teeth ensure clean cuts

Joint and strip cutter
Left-hand side used with a straightedge to cut joints between veneer sheets; also cuts precise veneer strips for use as edge banding. Right-hand side uses spacers to cut thin strips of veneer for fine inlay work; cuts with or across wood grain

Electric glue pot
Melts glue to correct consistency with electrically powered heater shell

Smoothing blade
Used like veneer hammer to press down veneer; works well with pressure-sensitive or fragile veneer

Glue brush
For spreading glue on substrate panel or veneer

Veneer press
For pressing veneer down on a substrate panel; features a base, pipe, clamps, pipe clamp saddles, and veneer press clamps. Components are bought as a kit and assembled by user to suit dimensions of panel

Router plane
Also known as a granny's tooth; small plane typically with a 1/4-inch-wide blade for clearing waste wood from grooves and recesses

Press screw
Clamping screw with removable swivel head used to make veneer presses and other jigs; available in 9- and 12-inch lengths

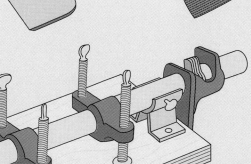

VENEERING

With the substrate panel secured in a bench vise, a woodworker presses down a strip of walnut veneer edge banding with a veneer hammer. The tool is pushed and pulled along the surface like a squeegee. The hammer's polished bronze face features a semicircular edge, which prevents scratching the veneer or snagging its edges.

CUTTING VENEER FROM SOLID LUMBER

1 Setting up the cut
To cut veneer on the band saw, first make a pivot block from two pieces of wood joined in a T, with the outer end of the shorter piece trimmed to form a rounded nose. Equip your saw with a ¾-inch resaw blade and install the rip fence on the table. Screw the pivot block to the fence so that the rounded tip is aligned with the cutting edge of the blade. Position the fence for the desired thickness of the veneer, typically ⅟₁₆ to ⅛ inch *(right)*.

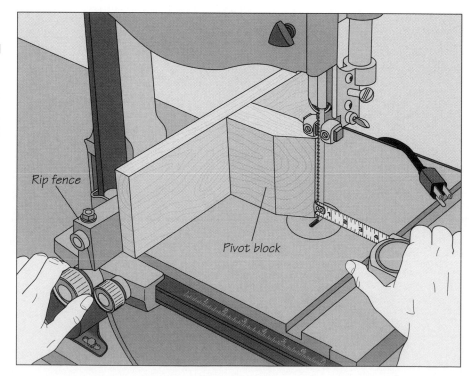

Rip fence

Pivot block

2 Cutting the veneer

Feed the workpiece into the blade with both hands, pressing the stock flush against the tip of the pivot block *(right)*. To prevent the blade from drifting off line, steer the trailing end of the workpiece. Near the end of the cut move to the back of the table and pull the stock past the blade to finish the cut. After each pass, run the cut edge of the workpiece across the jointer to ensure that one side of every piece of veneer is perfectly flat and smooth.

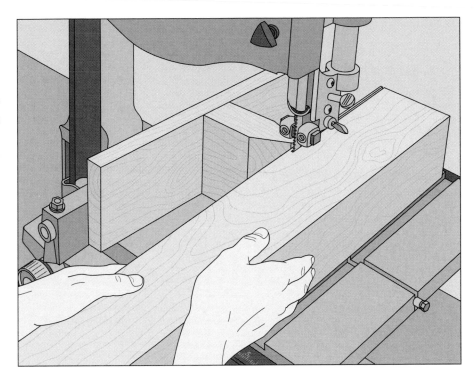

VENEER MATCHING

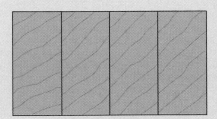

Slip match
Often used to dramatic effect; reduces distortion caused by light refraction problems when book-matching

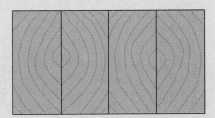

Book match
A repeating pattern in which adjoining sheets of veneer appear to radiate from the joint between them, like the pages of an open book

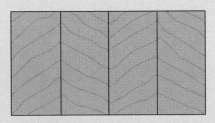

Herringbone
Veneer figure runs diagonally off the sheet, creating a zigzag effect

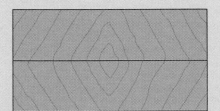

End-to-end
A mirror-image pattern featuring flat-cut veneers with prominent landscape figure

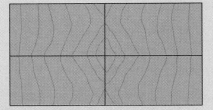

Butt-and-book match
Commonly used with butt, crotch, and stump veneers to create an unfolding, circular effect

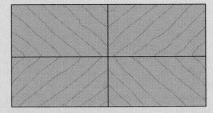

Reverse-diamond match
Features four sheets of veneer that appear to converge at the center

APPLYING VENEER TO A PANEL

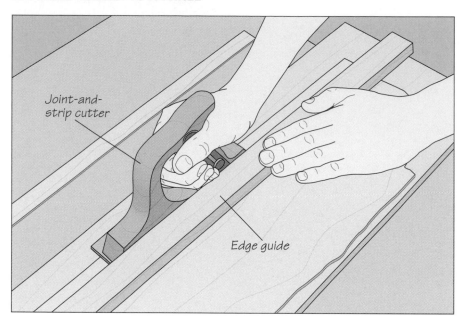

Joint-and-strip cutter

Edge guide

1 Cutting the veneer to size
You can use a joint-and-strip cutter to size your veneer for the surfaces of the panel. Mark the width of each strip so the veneer will be about ½ inch wider than the surface it will cover. Next, adjust the back cutter on the tool to a depth slightly greater than the thickness of the veneer. (Be sure to raise the front cutters above the sole of the tool.) For each cut, place the veneer on a scrap panel set atop a work surface and align an edge guide with your width mark. Holding the guide in place, push the cutter along the veneer. Press the edge of the tool against the edge guide throughout the cut *(left)*. Use the same technique to cut the veneer to length.

2 Applying edge banding
Start by applying banding to the edges and ends of the panel. Secure the work-piece in a vise with one edge facing up and apply a thin bead of glue to the surface. Use a small brush to spread the adhesive evenly, then center the banding on the edge. There should be at least ¼ inch over-hang on all sides. Lay a strip of wax paper over the banding and use three-way clamps to hold it in place, spacing the clamps at 6- to 8-inch intervals. Protecting the band-ing and the faces of the panel with wood pads, tighten the clamps *(right)* until a thin bead of glue squeezes out. (If you are using hot glue, apply the banding with a veneer hammer, as shown in the photo on page 122.) Once the glue has dried, trim excess banding with a laminate trimmer *(page 126)* or an edge trimmer. When using the latter, first trim the ends flush. To trim the edges, butt the trimmer's fence against the far end of the panel and push the tool along the edge *(inset)*. Repeat the process for the other edge.

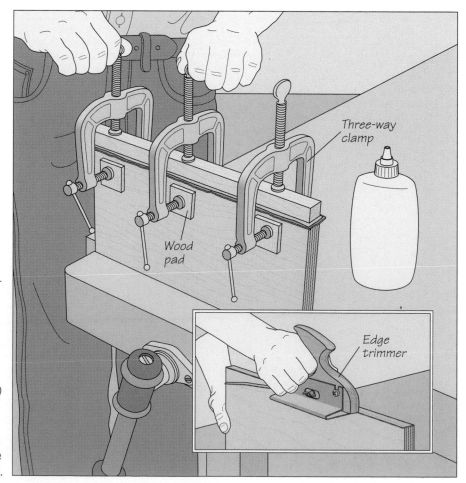

Three-way clamp

Wood pad

Edge trimmer

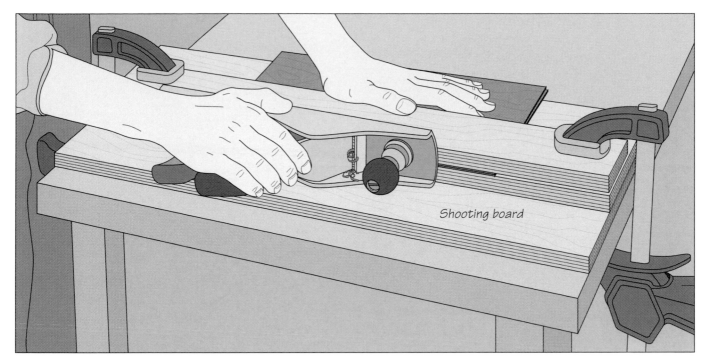

Shooting board

3 Edging the face veneer

The edges of adjoining sheets of face veneer must be perfectly straight if the two pieces are to butt together properly. To square them, you will need a shooting board. Cut three pieces of ¾-inch plywood slightly longer than the veneer. One piece must be wide enough to serve as a base for the other two pieces and a hand plane lying on its side. Place the two pieces of veneer face to face and sandwich them between the top two plywood boards so that the edges of the veneer are aligned and protrude by about ⅟₁₆ inch. Set the sandwich on top of the base board and clamp the entire assembly to a work surface. Run the plane along the shooting board from one end to the other to trim off the projecting veneer. Make sure you keep the sole of the plane flush against the edges of the top plywood pieces during the cut *(above)*.

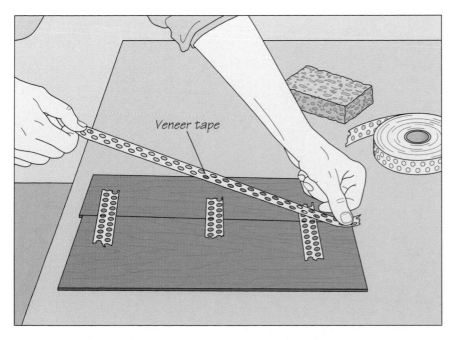

Veneer tape

4 Taping veneer sheets together

If you are using hot glue, secure the veneer sheets in place individually *(page 127)*. If you are applying more than one sheet of veneer to a panel face and using a veneer press to hold them down, tape the sheets together and glue them down as a unit. Do this by aligning the sheets edge to edge on a work surface, good-side up, to produce a visually interesting pattern. The combined length and width of the veneer should exceed the dimensions of the panel by about ½ inch. Once you have a satisfactory arrangement, moisten a few lengths of veneer tape with a damp sponge. Tape the sheets together across their joints at 6- to 8-inch intervals, then apply a strip of tape along each joint *(left)*. Press the tape firmly in place with a hand roller.

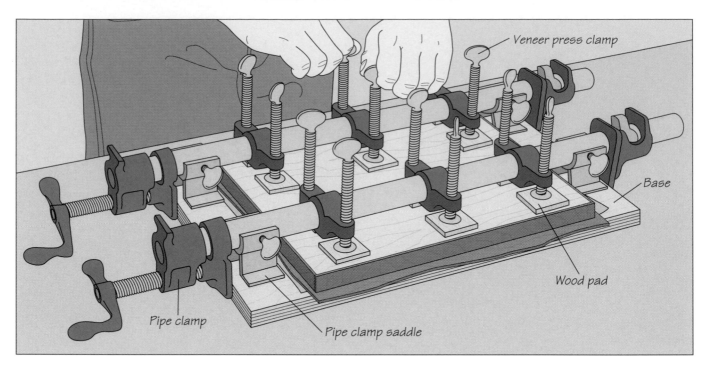

Veneer press clamp

Base

Wood pad

Pipe clamp

Pipe clamp saddle

5 Securing the veneer in place with a veneer press

Set the substrate panel face up on a work surface and apply a thin layer of glue. Handling the veneer gently, center the sheets on the panel. If you taped veneer sheets together, set them taped-side up. Make sure the veneer overhangs the edges of the panel evenly. If you are using a veneer press, assemble it following the manufacturer's instructions. Make sure the pipe clamps are secured to the base and the spacing between the saddles is slightly greater than the length of the panel. Set the panel on the base of the press, veneered-face down with a strip of wax paper between the veneered face of the panel and the base. Protect the upper face of the panel with wood pads. Tighten the press clamps one at a time *(above)* until a thin glue bead squeezes out from under the panel. Once the glue has dried, repeat the process for the other face of the workpiece.

6 Trimming the excess

Once the glue has cured—2 hours is the typical waiting period—trim the excess veneer. Secure the panel veneered-face up on a work surface. Butt wood scraps against the ends of the panel as cleats, then screw them in place. Lightly moisten any veneer tape and remove the strips with a scraper. Fit a laminate edge-trimmer with a flush-cutting bit, then rest the machine on the panel with the bit just clear of the excess veneer. Holding the trimmer with one hand and steadying the panel with the other, turn on the tool and guide it from one end of the workpiece to the other, cutting against the direction of bit rotation. Repeat for the other three edges of the panel. Flip the workpiece over and repeat the process *(right)*.

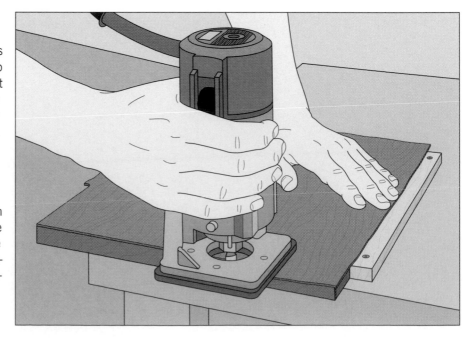

APPLYING FACE VENEER: AN ALTERNATE METHOD

1 Overlapping the veneer sheets

If you are applying veneer with hot glue and a veneer hammer, you can glue down the face pieces individually, rather than tape them together. Spread the glue on the underside of one sheet and the corresponding portion of the panel just prior to setting it down. Press the veneer down with the hammer *(photo, page 122)*. Apply the second sheet the same way so it overlaps the first near the middle of the panel by about ½ inch *(right)*; make sure the veneer overhangs the edges of the panel evenly.

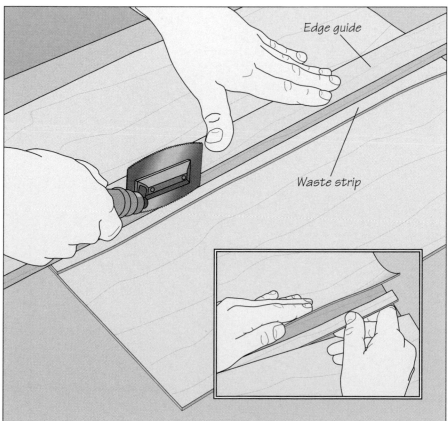

Edge guide

Waste strip

2 Removing the waste strips

Once both sheets are in place, use a veneer saw to cut away the excess veneer. Holding an edge guide on the panel within the area of overlap, draw the saw along the panel to cut through both sheets *(left)*. Remove the waste strip from the top piece, then heat the top sheet with a warm iron, carefully peel it up, and pull out the waste strip from the sheet underneath *(inset)*. The sheets should be butted together perfectly, resulting in a seamless joint. To finish the job, press a veneer hammer along the joint to squeeze out any excess glue. If the veneer lifts from the panel at the joint, reheat the glue with the iron and press the joint down with the hammer.

BUILD IT YOURSELF

VENEER PRESS

Made from plywood, hardwood, and six 9-inch-long press screws, the inexpensive shop-built veneer press shown below will work as well as a commercial model. The dimensions provided in the illustration will yield a press capable of veneering panels up to 16 by 24 inches.

Start by cutting the rails and stiles from hardwood. Bore three equidistant holes through the middle of each top rail, sized slightly larger than the diameter of the press screw collars you will

be using. Next, join the rails and stiles into two rectangular frames. The press in the illustration is assembled with open mortise-and-tenon joints *(inset)*, but through dovetails can also be used. Whichever joinery method you use, reinforce each joint with glue and three screws.

Now cut the pieces for the base and caul to size. Both are made from two pieces of ¾-inch plywood boards face-glued and screwed together. To assemble the press, set the two frames on their sides on a work surface, and

screw the base to the bottom rails, driving the fasteners from the bottom of the rails. Attach the press screws to the top rails by removing the swivel heads and collars, then tapping the collars into the holes in the top rails from underneath. Slip the threaded sections into the collars and reattach them to the swivel heads.

Use the press as you would the commercial model shown on page 126. Start applying pressure in the middle of the panel to prevent glue from becoming trapped.

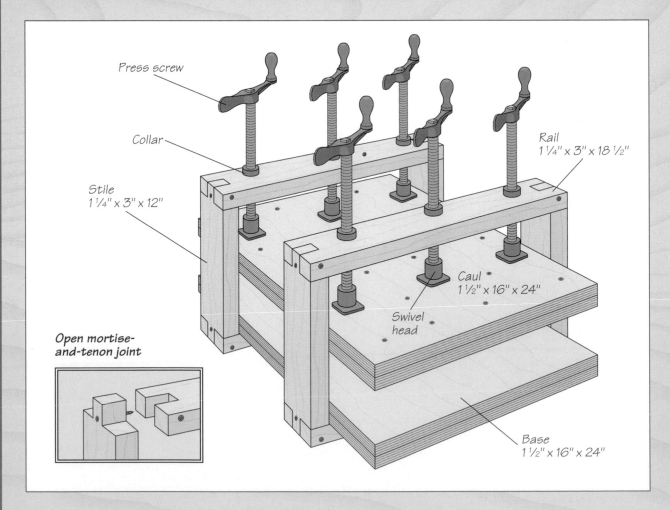

Press screw

Collar

Stile
1¼" x 3" x 12"

Rail
1¼" x 3" x 18½"

Caul
1½" x 16" x 24"

Swivel head

Open mortise-and-tenon joint

Base
1½" x 16" x 24"

USING A COMMERCIAL VACUUM PRESS

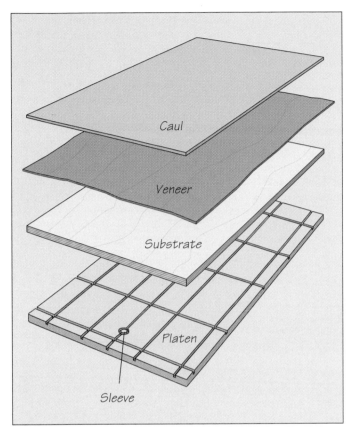

Caul

Veneer

Substrate

Platen

Sleeve

Veneering a panel

Featuring a sealed vacuum bag and a 5-cfm (cubic feet per minute) vacuum pump, the press shown below can exert pressure greater than 1000 pounds per square foot. The press works by withdrawing all the air from the bag; the resulting outside air pressure secures the veneer. To set up the press, cut the platen and caul to the same size as your substrate panel *(left)*. The platen should be made from medium density fiberboard or particleboard at least ¾ inch thick. Cut the caul from any type of manufactured board (other than plywood) at least ½ inch thick. To prepare the platen, round over its corners to avoid tearing the bag and cut a grid of grooves ⅛ inch deep and wide across its surface, spaced about 4 to 6 inches apart. Finally, bore a ⅝-inch hole 2 inches from one end of the platen and centered between its edges. Slip the sleeve supplied with the press into the hole. The sleeve will ensure a tight connection with the vacuum hose. Follow the manufacturer's instructions to use the press. For the model shown, insert the hose into the nipple in the bottom of the press bag. Then place the platen in the bag and slide the nipple into the platen sleeve. Set the substrate panel on a work surface, apply your glue, and lay the veneer on the substrate. Place a piece of wax paper over the veneer, rest the caul on top, and place the assembly atop the platen. Seal the bag, turn on the pump, and leave the assembly in the bag under pressure for the amount of time recommended by the manufacturer. Most vacuum presses will shut off when the appropriate pressure has been reached.

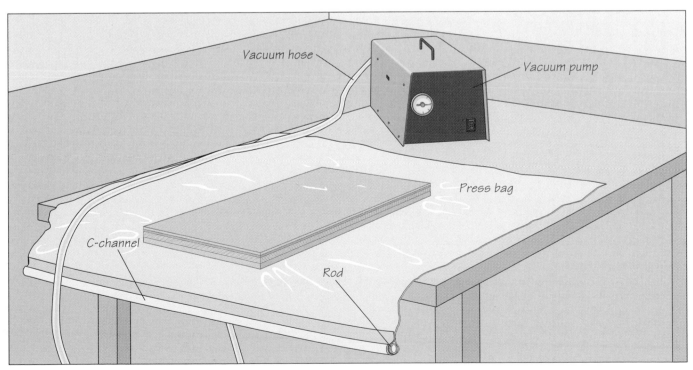

Vacuum hose

Vacuum pump

Press bag

C-channel

Rod

REPAIRING VENEER

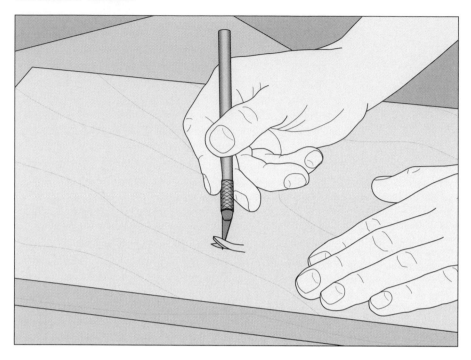

Extracting grit from under veneer
Specks of dirt or dust trapped under a sheet of veneer can prevent it from adhering properly to the substrate panel. To smooth out any resulting lumps, use a craft knife to make an angled incision around the problem area. Then peel back the flap of veneer *(left)* and use the knife to extract the foreign body. (A cut made with the grain will help to make the repair less visible.) Next, refasten the flap to the substrate. If you are using hot glue, pass a warm iron over the area and press the flap down with a veneer hammer. With other adhesives, apply a dab to the substrate and the underside of the flap and clamp it down *(page 131)*.

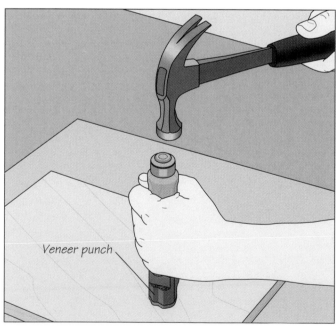

Veneer punch

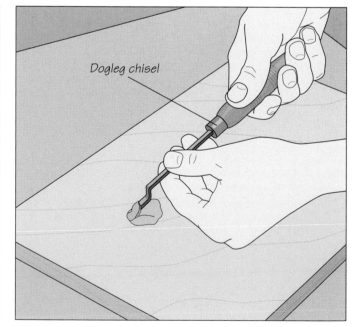

Dogleg chisel

Patching damaged veneer
You can repair a small section of damaged veneer by cutting it out with a veneer punch and replacing the piece with a patch of the same veneer species. If you used hot glue to adhere the veneer, first heat the damaged area with an iron before using the punch; this will make it easier to lift off the piece. To remove the damaged section, position the punch with the tool's cutting edge flat on the veneer. Strike the punch sharply with a hammer *(above, left)*. If the veneer does not come off in the punch, use a dogleg chisel to pare it away, being careful not to gouge the substrate panel *(above, right)*. Then punch out a piece of veneer to replace the damaged section, being sure to match the grain of the removed piece as closely as possible. Glue the patch in place.

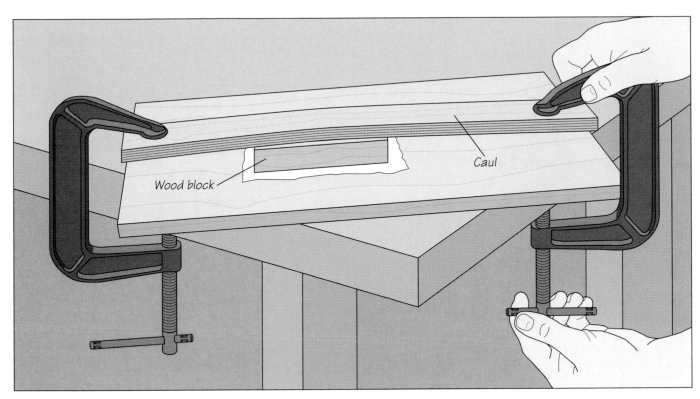

Wood block

Caul

SHOP TIP

Repairing air pockets (other than hot glues)
To remove air bubbles from under a veneer sheet that has not been stuck down with hide glue, first sand the surface with 80- to 100-grit sandpaper and spread a little water on the surface to moisten the veneer. This will cause the veneer to expand, allowing you to determine the exact location of the bubble. Slice through the bubble with a craft knife, cutting with the grain, and apply a dab of glue under the veneer with a needle-point glue injector. Clamp the veneer as you would if you were using hot glue, as shown above.

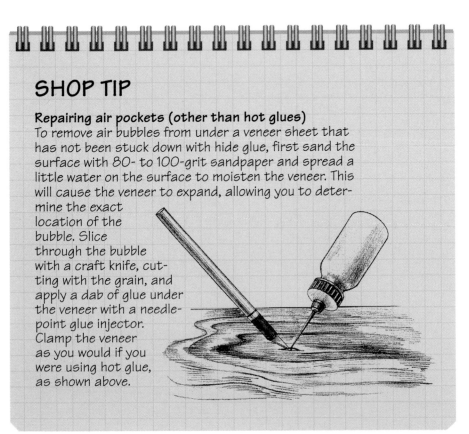

Repairing air pockets (hot glue)
If a section of veneer will not remain stuck down, and you are using hot glue, you can reclamp the section with a wood block and two C clamps. Simply reheat the bubbled section with a warm iron, press it down with a veneer hammer, and lay a piece of wax paper over it. Place the block on the paper and hold it down with two C clamps. If the block is farther from the edges of the panel than the clamps can reach, use a wood caul as long as the panel as a clamp extension. Place the caul on the wood block, install a C clamp at each end, and tighten the clamps until the caul is securely holding the block (above). (If you are not using hot glue, see the Shop Tip at left.)

MARQUETRY

Marquetry is the art of creating pictures with different-colored veneers. The technique is becoming increasingly popular, not only as a way of forming pictures in wood that are attractive in their own right, but also for embellishing an element of a piece of furniture, such as a tabletop, a drawer front, or a carcase panel.

The veneers are normally cut with a fret saw or a craft knife. For the novice, knife-cutting using the window method

Massachusetts craftsman Silas Kopf created the marquetry pattern on this cabinet from mahogany, maple, and a score of other woods. Kopf explains some of the challenges and the rewards of marquetry on page 12.

is recommended. The technique involves mounting a pattern on a sheet of waste veneer, called a waster. As you cut each section out of the picture, the hole in the waster serves as a template, or "window," for cutting the colored veneer you will use to fill the hole in the final picture. Once the veneer is cut, it is taped to the backside of the waster in its proper location. The process continues until the pattern is completed with all the veneers taped together. The picture is then glued to the substrate panel taped-side up. The tape will be sanded off, exposing the veneer.

Most marquetry kits, like the one shown below and on page 133, supply two patterns: One is taped to the waster and one remains intact as a master copy. The pictures and veneers are numbered to ease the assembly process.

USING A MARQUETRY KIT

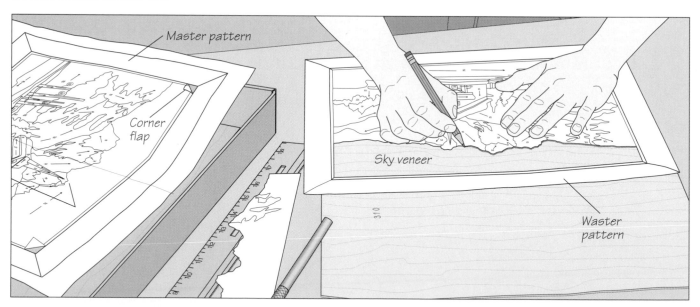

1 Tracing the main elements

Glue one pattern supplied with your kit to a sheet of waste veneer, or waster, at least as large as the pattern. Cut small flaps at the upper corners of the second pattern, your master copy. The flaps will help you in step 3 to align the master pattern with the waster. For now, start by cutting the main sections out of the waster one at a time—in this pattern, the sky and the water, slicing through the pattern and the backing veneer with a craft knife. To simplify the process, cut right through any elements, such as the tops of the trees, that overlap the section you are removing; these elements are added back in step 3. Once you have cut out the section, set the veneer that will fill the section on your work surface and position the waster over it. Arrange the waster so that the grain pattern of the veneer in the "window" is satisfactory. Then use a craft knife or a sharp pencil to trace the window's outline on the veneer *(above)*.

2 Taping main elements to the waster
Once the pattern has been traced on the veneer, cut it out with the craft knife. To ensure the edges are smooth, do not slice through the veneer in a single pass; instead, make several lighter cuts. Also, use a straightedge as a guide for straight cuts. Once the element has been cut out, place it in its window in the waster *(right)* and fasten it to the underside of the waster with veneer tape. Repeat steps 1 and 2 for each remaining main element of the picture.

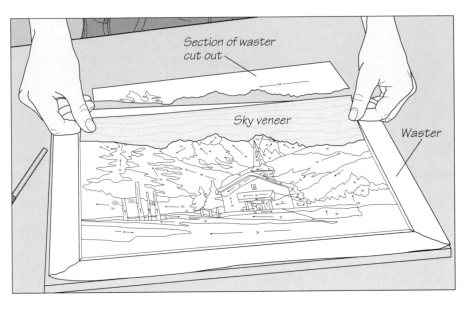

Section of waster cut out

Sky veneer

Waster

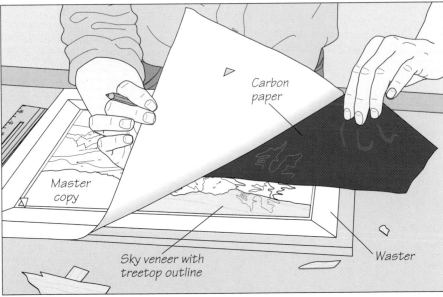

Carbon paper

Master copy

Sky veneer with treetop outline

Waster

3 Adding the overlapping elements
Once all the main elements of the pattern have been cut and taped to the waster, the elements that were cut in two in step 1 need to be reconstructed. This is done with carbon paper and the master pattern. Place a piece of carbon paper carbon-side down on the waster, then lay the master pattern over the carbon paper, using the corner flaps to help you align the two images. Use a pencil to trace the missing elements—in this illustration, the treetops. The carbon paper will transfer the outline onto the sky veneer already taped to the waster. Remove the master copy and carbon paper *(left, above)* and cut out a window for the treetops following the procedure described in step 1. Then cut the tree veneer and tape it to the waster as explained in step 2. Once all the overlapping elements of the pattern have been cut and taped, move on to the smaller elements of the pattern *(left, below)* until the picture is completed. To finish the marquetry, glue the picture tape-side up to a substrate as you would any face veneer *(page 125)*, and sand off the veneer tape.

INLAYING

Inlaid marquetry banding and a central marquetry inlay transform the simple mahogany panel shown at left. Whether you buy inlays or make them yourself, installation is the same: The piece is set into a recess cut in the surface of the wood and then sanded flush.

INSTALLING A MARQUETRY INLAY

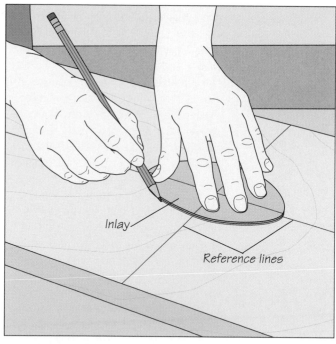

Inlay

Reference lines

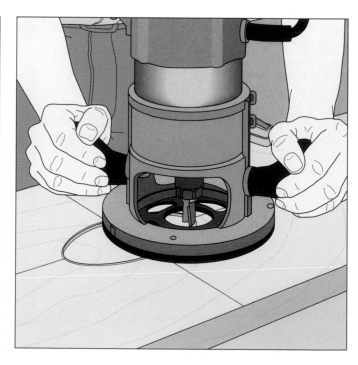

1 Routing the recess for the inlay
Once your inlay is ready to be installed, rout a recess for it in the center of the panel. First mark two lines across the panel that intersect at its center. Mark corresponding lines that cross at the center of the inlay, position the inlay on the panel so that the four reference marks line up, and outline the inlay on the surface with a pencil or knife *(above, left)*. Clamp the panel to a work surface. Install a straight bit in your router and set the depth of cut to the inlay thickness. (If you are installing shop-made inlay, which is thicker, set the bit depth slightly shallower than the inlay thickness.) Holding the router over the outline, turn on the tool and pivot the bit into the stock. Guide the router in small clockwise circles, moving against the direction of bit rotation *(above, right)*. Keep the base plate flat on the workpiece as you smooth the bottom of the recess, cutting to within 1⁄16 inch of the outline.

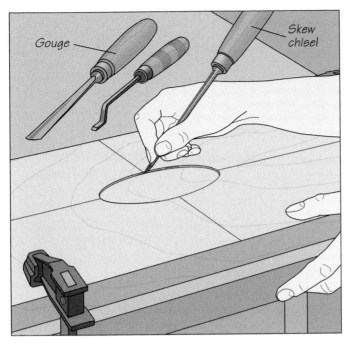

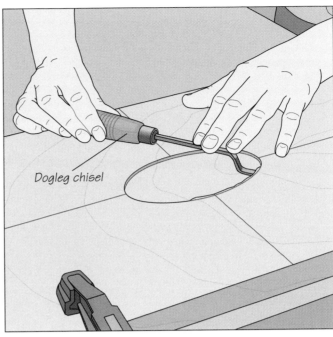

2 Trimming the edges of the recess

To complete the recess, cut to the marked outline with a skew chisel, a gouge, and a dogleg chisel. Start with the skew chisel, making an incision along the straighter sections of the outline to the depth of the recess *(above, left)*. Hold the chisel blade as you would a pencil, keeping the blade just inside the outline. On the tighter curves, use a gouge with the appropriate profile to score down to the recess depth. To finish, pare away the waste with a dogleg chisel. Holding the chisel bevel-up against the edge of the outline, apply light pressure to wedge out the waste *(above, right)*. Continue until all the waste has been removed. Clean any wood chips and dust out of the recess and test-fit the inlay.

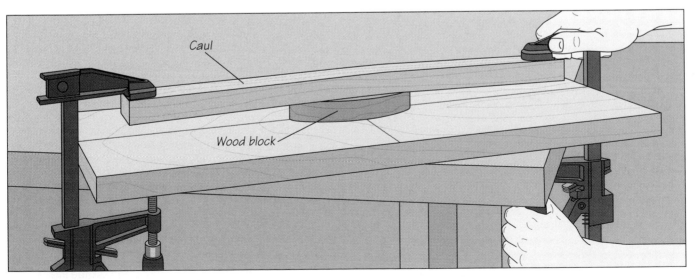

3 Installing the inlay

Spread a thin coating of glue in the recess and set the inlay in place—paper-side up if you are using commercial inlay. Cover the inlay with a piece of wax paper and cover it with a wood block that is slightly smaller than the inlay. Place a caul across the block, then clamp the ends of the board to secure the block *(above)*. When the glue has cured, remove the block and sand the inlay and surrounding wood to remove any paper covering and trim the inlay flush with the panel surface.

INLAY BANDING

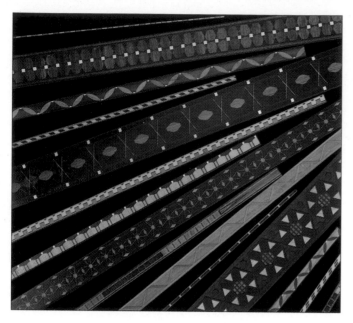

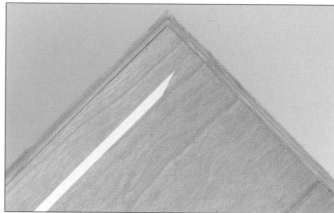

Inlay banding can take many forms, from plain wood strips cut in the shop to complex marquetry patterns. Shown at left is a sampling of what is available at specialty wood-working stores. Another option is solid metal banding, like the brass strip set into a tabletop shown above.

INSTALLING SHOP-MADE BANDING

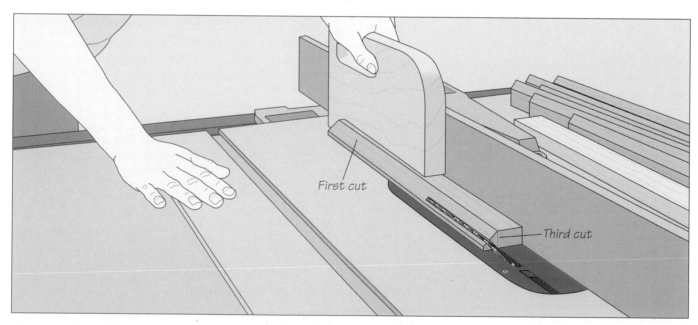

First cut

Third cut

1 Cutting the banding strips

One way to make your own banding involves cutting two contrasting woods into narrow strips and edge-gluing the strips together so their end grain creates an attractive pattern. The assembly is then sandwiched between sheets of veneer and crosscut to create patterned strips. One of the woods is cut into triangular lengths; the other is sawn into squares. Make the triangular pieces first, with three cuts on the table saw. For the first cut, position the rip fence to the left of the blade and set the cutting angle at 45°. Feed the board along the fence, beveling one face. Then flip the workpiece and saw an identical bevel on the other side *(above)*. For the final cut, adjust the blade to 90° and slice off the triangular strip, as represented by the dotted lines in the illustration. Use a push stick for all three passes. Cut the square pieces next, making sure the sides are equal to the angled sides of the triangular strips. Cut as many strips as you need, then saw them to the same length.

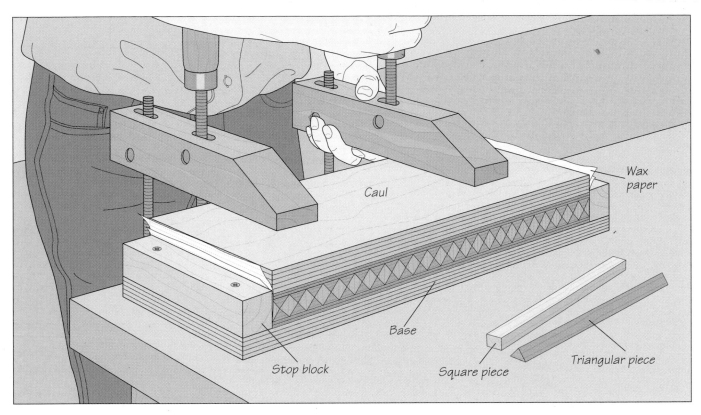

Wax paper

Caul

Base

Stop block

Square piece

Triangular piece

2 Gluing up the strips

The strips need to be edge-glued into a panel that can then be cut into lengths of banding. For glue up, use the set-up shown above: At each end of a plywood base, screw a stop block so the gap between the two equals the length of the banding you need. Cut a plywood caul and two sheets of veneer to the same length; their width should equal the length of the individual triangular and square pieces. Start by laying a sheet of wax paper and then at least two sheets of veneer on the base and spreading glue on the top surfaces of the veneers. Next, set a layer of the triangular strips flat side down on the veneer

from one stop block to the other. Spread a thin glue layer on the exposed sides of the triangles and lay in the squares, being sure to orient the grain of all the pieces in the same direction. At the ends of the assembly, in the gap against each stop block, place a trianglular piece cut from the same stock as the square piece. Complete the assembly by gluing down another layer of triangles and topping it off with at least two more veneer sheets. Place a sheet of wax paper over the veneer and lay the caul on the paper. Install two handscrews to clamp the assembly until the glue cures *(above)*.

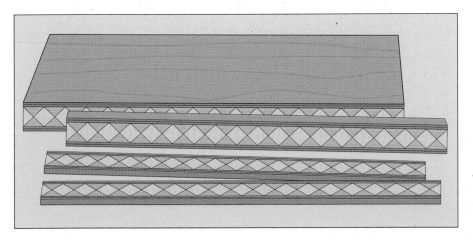

3 Slicing off the banding strips

Once the adhesive has cured, remove the clamps and sand off any squeeze-out. To complete the job, saw the glued-up panel into ⅛-inch-thick strips *(left)*.

APPLYING INLAY BANDING

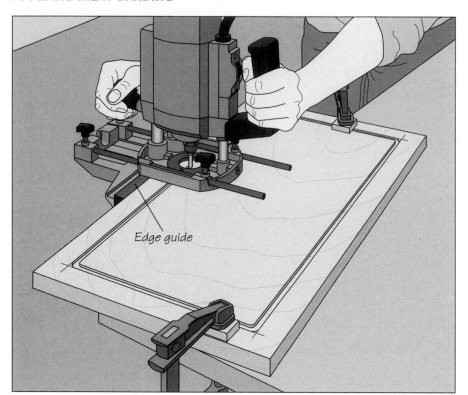

Edge guide

1 Routing a groove for the banding
Grooves for inlay can be cut with a router fitted with a straight bit the same width as the banding. If you are installing shop-made inlay, set the cutting depth slightly less than the thickness of the strips; the inlay will be sanded flush. For commercial banding, which is quite thin, make the cutting depth equal to the inlay thickness to minimize the sanding required. Outline the groove on your workpiece, adjust the router's edge guide to align the bit with the marks, grip the tool firmly, and cut the groove *(left)*. Square the corners with a chisel.

2 Setting the inlay in the groove
Cut the banding to fit in the groove, using your table saw for shop-made inlay, or a wood chisel for commercial banding. For the rectangular groove shown, make 45° miter cuts at the ends of the inlay pieces with a chisel *(right)*. Cut and fit one piece at a time, then spread a little glue on the underside of the inlay and insert it in the slot *(inset)*. Hold the banding in place with masking tape until the adhesive cures. If you are using marquetry inlay, try to maintain a continuous pattern, matching the design at each corner before cutting the pieces. Once the glue has dried, sand the surface to remove excess adhesive and trim the inlay flush with the surrounding surface.

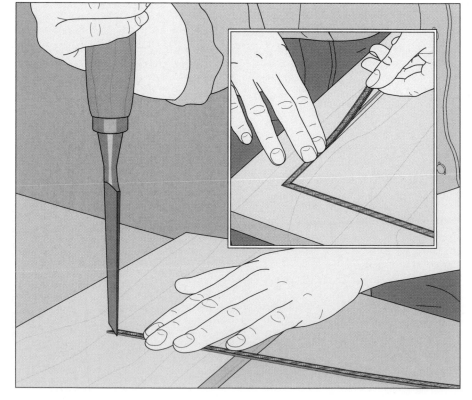

CUTTING A GROOVE FOR BANDING: AN ALTERNATE METHOD

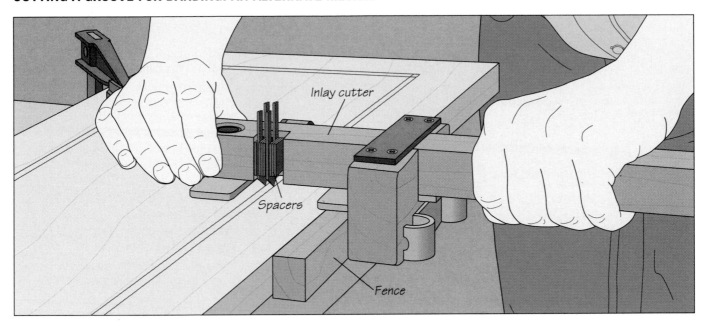

Inlay cutter

Spacers

Fence

1 Scoring the groove outline

You can use an inlay cutter rather than a router to score the outline of a groove and clear the waste with a router plane *(step 2)*. Following the manufacturer's instructions, make the width of the cut equal to the width of the banding and the cutting depth the same as the banding thickness. The cutter shown features metal spacers for setting the width of cut. Next, align the blades over the groove outline marks, butt the fence against the edge of the workpiece, and fix the fence in position. Holding the cutter as shown, lower the blades into the stock while butting the fence against the edge, and push the tool forward. Apply downward pressure to score the groove outline *(above)*, repositioning and reclamping the workpiece if necessary.

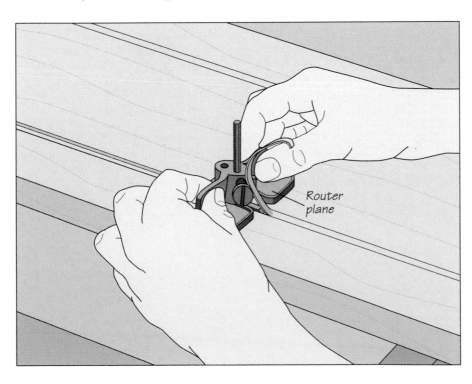

Router plane

2 Clearing the groove

To remove the waste from the groove, use a router plane with a blade no wider than the width of the groove. Set the depth of cut for the thickness of the inlay. Then, starting at one end of the groove, penetrate the stock with the blade within the scored lines until the sole of the plane is flat on the panel surface. Stand at one end of the panel and pull the plane toward you to clear the channel *(left)*. Repeat to clear the rest of the groove.

GLOSSARY

A-B-C-D

Adze: An ax-like tool with a curved blade used to carve out concave surfaces, such as chair seats.

Bendable plywood: A three-ply sheet material with a flexible inner core sandwiched between two outer layers with parallel grain.

Bending form: A jig commonly used with a tension strap to bend steamed, laminated, or kerfed wood.

Bird's-eye figure: Figure on plain-sawn and rotary-cut surfaces of a few species of wood—most notably maple—exhibiting numerous small, rounded features resembling birds' eyes. Commonly used as a veneer.

Bolt: A length of log that will be riven into appropriate-sized pieces for green woodworking projects.

Brake: A jig designed to hold thin or long stock for riving; commonly constructed from a forked tree limb and two straight limbs arranged in an X.

Burl veneer: Highly decorative veneer taken from bulges or irregular growths that form on the trunks of some species and on the roots of others.

Burr: A small ridge of metal that forms opposite the cutting edge of a tool blade during sharpening.

Cabriole leg: A type of furniture leg characterized by sweeping curves, imitating the graceful leg of a leaping animal.

Caul: Used in veneering, a board placed between clamps and the workpiece to distribute clamping pressure.

Checking: A lumber defect in which splits develop across the growth rings because of uneven shrinkage of wood during seasoning.

Compression: In steam bending, stresses on the inside curve of the bend that squeeze the wood fibers.

Coopering: The technique of making wooden barrels from tapered, beveled staves; also, creating curved panels by edge-gluing a series of wood strips with beveled edges.

Crotch veneer: Veneer cut from the fork of a tree trunk.

E-F-G-H-I-J

Eye: In carving, a small hole where two elements of a design overlap to create the illusion of depth.

Figure: The distinctive pattern produced on a wood's surface by the combination of annual growth rings, deviations from regular grain, rays, knots, and coloration.

Fixed end stop: In steam bending, a hardwood block bolted to each end of a metal tension strap to hold a bent workpiece in place and prevent it from splitting along the outside of the bend.

Flake figure: A decorative pattern in wood consisting of irregularly shaped, elongated areas running parallel to each other across the grain. Highly prized as veneer.

Flitch: A section of a log cut in order to extract the best figure and highest yield of veneers.

Froe: An L-shaped tool with a beveled blade that is struck by a club to rive, or split, green wood.

Froe club: A wooden striking tool used with a froe to rive green wood; typically hewn from the limb of a dense, close-grained hardwood.

Glut: A wooden wedge used for splitting logs.

Grain: The direction, size, arrangement, or quality of the elements in wood; specifically, the alignment of wood fibers with respect to the axis of the tree trunk.

Green wood: Freshly felled or unseasoned wood.

Hot glue: Any of several types of glue, including varieties made from animal hides, that are heated before use and then harden upon cooling; traditionally used in veneering.

Inlay: A decorative strip of metal, wood, or marquetry that is glued into a groove cut into a workpiece.

K-L-M-N-O

Kerf bending: The technique of bending wood by cutting a series of equally spaced kerfs in one face of a workpiece so that it will bend more easily.

Laminate bending: Bending wood by resawing it into thin, flexible strips and then gluing up the strips around a curved form.

Marquetry: Decorative inlay work done with veneers, metals, or various other materials; pieces are formed into patterns or pictures.

Moisture content: The amount of water contained in wood, expressed as a percentage of the weight of completely dry wood.

Molding head: A solid metal wheel that attaches to the arbor of a stationary saw and holds sets of shaped knives for milling wood.

Mottled figure: A type of broken stripe figure with occasional interruptions of curly figure.

P-Q-R

Piping: In carving, a cylindrical, tube-like element designed to suggest folds in leaves or linen.

Plain-sawn lumber: Lumber that has been sawn so that the boards' wide surfaces are tangent to the annual growth rings. Also known as flat-sawn lumber when referring to softwood; see *quartersawn lumber*.

Quartersawn lumber: Lumber that has been sawn so the wide surfaces of the boards intersect the growth rings at angles between 45° and 90°. Also known as vertical-grained lumber when referring to softwood; see *plain-sawn lumber*.

Quirk: On a molding, a narrow, flat recess that borders a curved element.

Relief carving: A style of carving that elevates the design into prominence by cutting away the surrounding wood.

Resawn lumber: Lumber that has been ripped into thin strips, often for laminate bending.

Riving: The technique of splitting wood from a log with a sledgehammer and wedges or with froes and clubs so that the wood separates along the fibers.

Rotary-cut veneer: A continuous sheet peeled from a log by rotating it against a stationary knife on a lathe.

S-T

Seasoning: The process or technique of drying wood.

Slipstone: Small sharpening stone available in various shapes and sizes typically used to remove burrs and hone inside bevels of edge tools.

Steam bending: The technique of softening wood for bending by subjecting it to steam and heat and then bending it around a curved form.

Story pole: A shop-made measuring gauge used to determine the location of the joints in a project, such as a stool or chair.

Strop: A strip of leather dressed with a fine abrasive to polish the cutting edges of gouges, chisels, and other carving tools.

Supported steam bending: Bending steamed wood on a form equipped with a tension strap; typically done with air-dried stock. See *unsupported steam bending*.

Sweep: The degree of curvature across the blade of a carving tool.

Temper: The degree of hardness of a metal, primarily steel, brought about by controlling the heating and cooling processes.

Tension strap: In steam bending, a steel band with fixed hardwood end stops positioned against the outer curve of the workpiece; helps prevent the wood from splitting by transforming the tension forces in the outer curve of the bend into compression forces on the inside curve.

Torsion box: In laminate bending, a two-piece bending form with curved plywood panels supported by ribs, used to bend large laminates or veneered plywood panels.

U-V-W-X-Y-Z

Unsupported steam bending: Bending steamed wood with only a bending form; typically used with green wood for complex bends in more than one plane. See *supported steam bending*.

Veneer: A thin layer or sheet of wood sawn, sliced, or rotary cut from a log or flitch.

Veneer matching: The technique of creating interesting and attractive patterns with like-figured sheets of veneer.

INDEX

Page references in *italics* indicate an illustration of subject matter. Page references in **bold** indicate a Build It Yourself project.

ACKNOWLEDGMENTS

The editors wish to thank the following:

WORKING GREEN WOOD
Anglo-American Enterprises Corp., Somerdale, NJ; Drew Langsner, Marshall, NC;
Lee Valley Tools Ltd., Ottawa, Ont.; Record Tools Inc., Pickering, Ont.; Sears, Roebuck and Co.,
Chicago, IL; Woodcraft Supply Corp., Parkersburg, WV

BENDING WOOD
Delta International Machinery/Porter-Cable, Guelph, Ont.; Mike Dunbar, Portsmouth, NH;
Michael Fortune, Toronto, Ont.; Lee Valley Tools Ltd., Ottawa, Ont.; Oak Park Enterprises, Ltd.,
Elie, Man.; Dave Sawyer, South Woodbury, VT; Joan Sawyer, Rancho Santa Fe, CA; Sears,
Roebuck and Co., Chicago, IL; Stanley Tools, Division of the Stanley Works, New Britain, CT;
Vacuum Pressing Systems Inc., Brunswick, ME; John Wilson, The Home Shop, Charlotte, MI

CARVING
Adjustable Clamp Co., Chicago, IL; Ian Agrell, Sausalito, CA; American Tool Cos., Lincoln, NE;
Martha Collins, Lost Mountain Editions, Ltd., Sequim, WA; Albert Constantine and Son Inc., Bronx, NY;
Delta International Machinery/Porter-Cable, Guelph, Ont.; Bob Jardinico, Plymouth, MA;
Leonard Lee, Ottawa, Ont.; Lee Valley Tools Ltd., Ottawa, Ont.; Alain Morcel, Les Réalisations
Loeven-Morcel, Montreal, Que.; Richards Engineering Co., Ltd., Vancouver, B.C.;
Sandvik Saws and Tools Co., Scranton, PA; Stanley Tools, Division of the Stanley Works,
New Britain, CT; Woodcraft Supply Corp., Parkersburg, WV

VENEER, INLAY, AND MARQUETRY
Adjustable Clamp Co., Chicago, IL; A & M Wood Specialty Inc., Cambridge, Ont.;
Great Neck Saw Mfrs. Inc. (Buck Bros. Division), Millbury, MA; Albert Constantine and Son Inc.,
Bronx, NY; Delta International Machinery/Porter-Cable, Guelph, Ont.; Silas Kopf, Northampton, MA;
Lee Valley Tools Ltd., Ottawa, Ont.; Stanley Tools, Division of the Stanley Works, New Britain, CT;
Vacuum Pressing Systems Inc., Brunswick, ME; The Woodworker's Store, Rogers, MN

The following persons also assisted in the preparation of this book:

Donna Curtis, Lorraine Doré, Mike Dunbar, Graphor Consultation, Geneviève Monette

---

PICTURE CREDITS

Cover Bill Truslow
6, 7 Martin Fox
8, 9 Ed Homonylo
10, 11 Robert Holmes
12, 13 Kevin Downey
15 Martin Fox
41 David Allen
57 David Allen
70 Robert Holmes
76 Courtesy Veritas Tools, Inc.
101 Robert Holmes
132 David Ryan
136 *(left)* Courtesy Lee Valley Tools Ltd.